QLIPHOTH OPUS III

QLIPHOTH OPUS III

-The Cycles Ov Primal Kaos-

Edited by Edgar Kerval

Nephilim Press
2013

Qliphoth Opus III
-The Cycles Ov Primal Kaos-

ISBN: 978-0-9830639-8-8

Published by Nephilim Press
A division of Nephilim Press LLC
www.nephilimpress.com

Copyright © 2015 Nephilim Press and Edgar Kervall. All rights reserved.

No part of this publication may be reproduced, stored in a retrieval system, or transmitted, in any form or by any means, without the prior written permission of the publisher, nor be otherwise circulated in any form of binding or cover other than that in which it is published and without a similar condition being imposed on the subsequent purchaser.

Qliphoth journal is a grimoire focusing the diverse paths of magick in its entire splendor. Our main focus is to cross the paths of knowledge via praxis, ritual and gnosis, working intensely in each one of the volumes offered here. Through this third opus called *The Cycles Ov Primal Kaos*, the focus is to go back to such primal states of consciousness through the methods of atavistic resurgence awakening the immortal essence of the self, through the development of our own divinity with direct experience with spirits, servitors, guardians, and loas of our own temples. It is there where the sacred nectars are consumed… where the secret seed incarnates, through the hidden labyrinths and the secret wisdom veiled by the tendrils of Trans human entities… So then, we enter once again *The Cycles Ov Primal Kaos*.

—Edgar Kerval, 2013

This opus III, *The Cycles Of Primal Kaos*, is dedicated to the Red Gods and spirits from zothiria for their cooperation and influx of primal essences. To Nephilim Press for its incredible support, to each one of the authors whose contributions are compiled herein, and specially to Sean Woodward and Kyle Fite for the support and brotherhood throughout the years. Finally to my brother Phil Brito for infinite support through hard times here in Colombia!

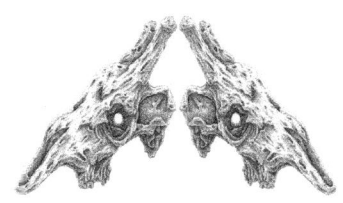

Contents

Qlipothic Initiation 1
Asenath Mason

The Path of Nasa & Alchemical Catharsis 15
S. Connolly

Unguentum Sabbati 23
Matthew Venus

Qalilitu: The Evil Mermaid From The Bloody Water Of Gamaliel 31
Daemon Barzai

Becoming Hoodoo Part 3 35
Kyle Fite

The Serpent's Servants: Disciples of Ain 45
Matthew Wightman

The Living Atua Of The Carrefour Tarot 55
Sean Woodward

Sigil Inversion And Qliphothic Gestalt 73
Robert Podgurski

Kali: The Womb Of Death And Void 87
Daemon Barzai

Thantifaxath: A Recollection 91
Albert Petersen

The Oracle Of The Void
(Amprodias Exploration in the 11th Tunnel).........................99
Edgar Kerval

Ignition Of The Black Flame 103
David Eosphorus Maples

Hell's Rapture... 113
Mica Gries

Ielejkjn Heleikinn– Necromancy.................................. 125
Ljóssál Loðursson

Illustrations

Conversation VVith Unholy Guardian Angel By Rafal Kosela xi

2007 e .v-by william Ba:e Hale. xii

Thaumiel Seal by edgar kerval 8

Qabalistic Tree by Aseanth Mason 11

nasa putrefaction by S. connolly 18

saturn4 by S.connolly 19

Another Round by Isabele Gaborit 21

Baphometis by Matthew Venus 30

Qalilitu Seal by Daemon Barzai. 32

Gran Bwa by kyle fite. 37

Hoodoo entry point by kyle fite. 39

Baptism by Kyle fite 42

Dharmakara by kyle fite 44

Serpent by Matthew Wightman. 51

The Heirdom by Rafal kosela 53

The Initiate of the Northern Cross by Sean Woodward. 60

Carrefour Syzygies by Sean Woodward 63

The Twins of the Ritual Design by Sean Woodward 68

Master of the Words of the Island Under The Sea by Sean Woodward... 72

Closure 2 by Robert Podgurski 74

Gargophias by Robert Podgurski 78

Spares gridlike sigils by Robert Podgurski. 80

Muses chart by Robert Podgurski.............................. 81

A.Y.V.V.V.A.S by rafal kosela................................ 85

Candlemass by Isabel gaborit................................. 95

Amprodias Sigil by edgar kerval 100

Amprodias Rising by edgar Kerval........................... 101

Untitled by Barry willliam Hale 102

Veve of Legba by edgar kerval 107

Veve of Baron Samedi 108

Veve of Kalfu by edgar kerval 108

Zobop Mosquito.. 110

Bindu Trident 110

Veve of Erzuli Dantor by edgar kerval 111

everything must die exept my love for you by isabele gaborit.......... 117

from the bonefire of our love by isabele gaborit 122

666+156=93 by rafal kosela.................................. 124

Heleikinn– Necromancy....... Ljóssál Loðursson.................. 128

Rúnarsteinn Kalleby –Kalleby Runic Stone..................... 135

Conversation VVith Unholy Guardian Angel
By Rafal Kosela

2007 e .v
By william Bare Hale

Qlipothic Initiation

Asenath Mason

Initiation in itself is a process that is often misinterpreted or misunderstood by individual practitioners, and it also raises a lot of controversy, as initiatory systems are used by many magical groups to create artificial hierarchies. There are many definitions of "initiation." This largely depends on esoteric school or magical system which provides grounds for the change in the spiritual level of the initiate—as initiation is, above all, a change, transformation, transition from one level to another. This change occurs in many different areas and on many different levels. In initiatory systems used by esoteric groups and magical orders, this usually includes a particular ceremony that represents the rite of passage through which the initiate obtains a higher status. This is also connected with obtaining access to knowledge that until that moment was beyond the initiate's reach. True initiation, however, is not a singular ceremony but a process that lasts for a certain period of time and confronts the adept with a particular mystical experience. This experience is personal illumination, alchemical transmutation, and spiritual transition that transforms the initiate's consciousness through personal process in which the whole life and perception of the world is changed.

Here we have to stress that there are many different levels of this "mystical experience," and practically every day we are faced with events that influence and change our consciousness to a lesser or greater extent. Life itself confronts us with challenges that work as "lesser initiations." But true initiation involves changes significant enough to turn the whole world upside down. The world around is shattered, all beliefs and values are questioned and lose their meaning, and the initiate feels like the whole life is falling apart, while he can only watch helplessly, without being able to stop this. In this process the initiate often goes through a breakdown, a dark night of the soul, when the ego is temporarily dissolved and consciousness is being rebuilt in order to enter the further stage of spiritual ascent.

The loss of ego creates inner emptiness, which often results in psychic and emotional damage: depression, despair, lack of self-confidence, inability of self-judgment, or fear of the surrounding world. This is experienced as loss of something undefined but valuable, a desperate longing that cannot be suppressed or satisfied. Very often the initiate does not recognize what is going on and fails to pass the initiatory test, thus being unable to progress from the darkness of depression to the light of illumination. This failure may end in further mental disorders or suicide, as the person does not see the light in the surrounding blackness and despair. This condition is not necessarily triggered by magical practice. Radical changes in consciousness may be caused by many different factors and affect everyone. Nevertheless, the very essence of all magical practices is to initiate certain changes in the adept's consciousness; therefore, when taking first steps on a magical path, we have to be aware of consequences. It is for a reason that magical initiation has been described in many cultures and traditions by means of death symbolism. For instance, candidates for shamans were torn apart by spirits and their body parts were devoured in the initiatory process. In alchemical allegory of initiation, we encounter the concept of *Nigredo*, the blackening, which is the first phase of alchemical process in which all ingredients are dissolved and left to putrefy. In psychological terms, this concept corresponds to depression, the dark night of the soul, and in magical symbolism, this signifies the death of the soul which is to be reborn and empowered through the initiatory process. What is more, when entering the "death stage," the alchemical *Solve* (dissolution), we have no certainty how it will end, if we will succeed through the black phase and enter the stage of *Coagula* (coagulation, binding), in which emptiness will be filled by power and self-confidence. Initiation is a test, and whether we pass it successfully or not depends only on our inner strength, determination and self-awareness. A person unprepared for such an ordeal has little chances of success, as this confrontation usually involves all that is feared, rejected, seen as repulsive or forbidden. It is the descent into personal "Underworld," confrontation with your own "dark side."

Qlipothic initiatory system is based on the Qabalistic Tree of Night, known as the Tree of Death. However, it is not possible to speak about the Tree of Death without speaking of the Tree of Life, as they are both complementary sides of the same model of the universe, two parts of the greater whole. Initiation through the Qlipothic Tree is at the same time initiation through its bright side. It is the descent into the depths of the soul through successive levels of the Tree of Death, representing the alchemical Solve, and it is the reconstruction of the soul through Sephirothic light of the alchemical Coagula. The initiate starts the journey by entering the Nightside through gateways hidden in the physical world (Lilith) and ascends through the astral/moon plane (Gamaliel, Samael and A'Arab Zaraq), solar sphere (Thagirion, Golachab, Gha'agsheblah), and stellar realm (Satariel, Ghagiel, Thaumiel). On the material plane the initiate learns the foundations of the path and opens the gateways to the Nightside. Ordeals of the astral realm bring confrontation with the unconscious, thoughts, feelings, and dreams. In the solar sphere the initiate unites with personal Daimon and learns the meaning of Godhood. This brings understanding of human limitations and possibilities of spiritual ascent. The Eye of Lucifer opens in the soul and all illusions of the world are shattered. Gazing into Infinity, the initiate forms his own definition of Creation. Finally, the path leads into the Void, the very source of all manifestation, the womb of the Dragon.

Each successive initiation on the path is different and each brings a new transformation, new change in consciousness of the initiate. Step by step we become completely different persons, as if we were born anew. Also, each initiatory ordeal confronts us with new challenges, and we have to be careful and aware that each test can be failed and we might lose ourselves in realms of darkness. Then it might take years, a lifetime, or even many incarnations before we find our way back on the right track. The path through the realms of the Qlipoth is harsh, winding, disappearing in the blackness of the Night. Results of magical work are fast, but it is also easy to lose everything any time.

Qlipothic initiation is also something that we have to deal with on our own. It is a part of the left-hand-path tradition, which is in its essence solitary and isolated. Ritual groups and left-hand-path magical orders usually have a short existence, as they gather strong-willed, self-reliant individuals, focused on their personal ascent and development of powerful personality, who are not necessarily able to work in a group or find themselves subjected to any hierarchy. It is even more difficult to find a genuine left-hand-path teacher, an advanced initiate, who might be interested in passing the knowledge to others. If we reject self-proclaimed spiritual masters, whose egos thrive on greed or delusions, we are left with the conclusion that the Left Hand Path is a solitary road, and it should be approached as such indeed. The best way to progress with the left-hand-path initiatory systems is to work on your own, with gods, spirits, and all other manifestations of the current as your guides and allies. A teacher or mentor can only point you at the right direction, while the main core of the work is the combination of self-knowledge and individual experience. It is our personal "dark side" that is confronted, and only we alone are able to progress successfully through the whole process, and it is our personal, inner Daimon who acts as the true initiator. Magical practices release forces that trigger this transformation—manifesting both on the level of consciousness and in the events of the physical universe. Initiatory ordeal usually occurs completely unexpected, when we do not feel ready for it. But then, the only way to successfully emerge from the ordeal is to confront it, as in fact, it would not be happening if we were not open for it and ready to receive it.

It may come at a moment of reading a novel as easily as when we are involved in a magical ritual. Quoting the words of Stephen Edred Flowers from his *Hermetic Magic,* "True initiation is not the kind of thing a member of the elect might choose to do in the same way one might choose to go to the movies on Saturday night. It is not simply a matter of desire, but of Necessity. It is a matter of pure survival for one who is truly elect."

Initiation also does not happen in a single ritual. It is the effect of conscious and willed life experience, combined with moments in which understanding of that experience is assimilated. True initiation is not an act of magic; it is a process in which the whole life is turned into the Great Work of magic. Through this process the initiate learns that the purpose of the path is not to *do* magic but to *become* magic. Quoting the same author again, "Rarely is true initiation coincidental with ceremonial activity."

Qlipothic Initiation

The Left Hand Path is based on individual approach and views man as an isolated, independent, self-reliant being. By taking successive initiatory steps on the path, we build a powerful personality, charismatic and self-confident. The greatest part of the work relies on our judgment, intuition, experience, and expectations. Initiatory path is personal, and initiatory experience manifests through the most personal and intimate spheres of our lives. Everyone has to face their own "demons:" personal taboos, weaknesses, obsessions, inhibitions, fears, fascinations, fantasies, etc. By facing and understanding them, we learn how to use them as tools of our personal spiritual evolution—we transcend barriers and limitations of human nature, our consciousness expands and we become "god-like." Each aspiring initiate would like to know what exactly happens on each initiatory level, what we might expect, and how to prepare for all this. This is not possible. All descriptions of initiations that are found in books are usually obscure, abstract and vague because spiritual initiation is a unique experience for each initiate and no one will ever experience personal godhood in the same way as another person. Therefore, there are thousands of descriptions and explanations of what "self-deification" means and none of them can be dismissed as false, as well as none of them is correct. This is because there is no objective "Truth" to find and no universal system producing the same results for everyone who steps onto the path. A left-hand-path initiate sees himself as God in potential, but the path is the process of continuous learning and we never know what awaits us on initiatory levels that we have not reached yet. One "self-deification" is never the same as another. There are certain shared concepts in the Qlipothic initiatory models but their meaning is always different for everyone, e.g., Gamaliel will confront you with your sexuality, but your sexual issues will not be the same as for another adept who works with this Qlipha or even with the same techniques and rituals. Samael will bring forth issues of doubt and insanity, but this will mean something completely different for you than for anyone else. In the same way, the experience of Thaumiel, which is the highest initiatory level on the Tree, is unique for each adept. Gods and entities who teach the gnosis of the Left Hand Path set up unique tests and challenges for everyone, depending on your personal limitations, and you may have glimpses of your personal "godhood" at various stages of the path, but the true meaning of "self-deification" is a mystery that can be only solved by experience.

Many practitioners, undergoing the harsh tests of the initiatory ordeal, have a tendency to stop doing magical work when they see things going bad for them in their everyday lives. This is not a good solution. Continuation of magical work aids and empowers initiation, enhances its effect. The purpose of the whole work is the very change, transformation that occurs through transition to another level of spiritual ascent, development of certain skills and abilities. Each initiatory experience also brings you closer to your personal Daimon. The only help and assistance that can be given to an aspiring initiate on the Qlipothic path is preparation for what may happen. This is exactly the role of all initiatory models and maps in magical systems—such as the Qlipothic Tree of Knowledge.

Tree of Qlipoth is a dark, demonic anti-structure to the Tree of Life. Instead of 10 Sephiroth, representing Light and Divine Order, we have 11 Qliphoth (sing. Qlipha), or "shells," which embrace all conceptions, energies, forces, etc., that were left out of the Divine Structure. The Qliphoth are usually believed to constitute the debris left over from the act of Creation. They are demons and dark forces that were banished from the Tree of Life through cleansing processes, but are constantly tormenting man from their own demonic anti-world. Throughout the ages, Qabalists believed that the Qlipoth represent the concept of Satan, the Adversary. There are even theories which claim that the name of the Lord of Darkness is HVHI, the name of God ("Jehovah") spelt backwards. Beyond the Tree of Life and the Tree of Qlipoth exists the Void, the eternal, limitless and timeless essence of the Dragon, the force behind all Creation and all Destruction. The gateway to this force is sometimes believed to exist in the hidden Sephirah Daath which exists on both Trees and connects them through the Abyss. But the actual gateway to the Void exists in the 11th Qlipothic sphere, Thaumiel, where Lucifer resides on His Throne, watching over the worlds of both Darkness and Light.

There are many Qabalistic theories concerning the Qlipoth, their creation, powers and purpose. One of these theories, for example, ascribes the creation of the Qlipoth to the judging side of God, Geburah. Geburah broke out of the original unity of the Sephiroth, declaring, "I shall rule." It was forced back into balance, but certain parts of this force were liberated and never re-joined the Sephirothic structure. These parts turned against God and began their own emanations, which the Qabalists describe as mockery against the Divine Worlds and anti-structure to the Divine

Order. While there are 10 Sephiroth to reflect the perfection of God, there are 11 emanations in the dark anti-worlds. The last Qlipha, Thaumiel, is split in two and denies the concept of Salvation through unity with God. Instead, the initiate of the Qlipothic Tree is given a choice to step out of Creation and enter the Void, through the 11th Qlipothic level, the Throne of Lucifer. The Qlipoth are ruled by the primordial demonic couple Lucifer and Lilith, sometimes it is Samael and Lilith, and sometimes these two demonic rulers are believed to be one and the same. The fall of Geburah is described in a manner that is reminiscent of the rebellion of Lucifer against God and his Divine Order.

Another popular theory was proposed by Isaac Luria, the famous sixteenth-century Qabalist. According to his doctrine, Tree of Qlipoth was formed as a result of *Tzimtzum*, the primordial self-withdrawal of God who "made space" for subsequent Creation, thus providing foundations for the 10 Sephiroth. Then, God filled the Sephiroth with Divine light, but the overflow of the force caused the vessels to break and from Binah down to Yesod, Sephirothic spheres were shattered. The shards of the broken vessels fell down, splintering into innumerable fragments, creating realms of impurity known as the Qlipoth. Most of Divine sparks returned to higher spiritual realms, but some of them were imprisoned in Qlipothic realms.

According to Lurianic Kabbalah, the greatest task of man is to recreate the Divine Order by liberating the sparks of light from the kingdoms of impurity. This process, known as "tikkun," was initiated by the Divine force itself, but it was broken by the fall of Adam. Human souls were separated from the higher realms and, since then, they cannot regain their primordial unity. These souls are the very sparks imprisoned in the Shells, and their salvation cannot take place without the work of man. That is why man was created and placed in the realm of the Shells, the first and lowest of the Qabalistic worlds.

The word "Qlipha" itself literally means "shell" or "husk." It is but one of possible meanings, as it can also be translated as "cave" or "womb," which associates the realm of Qlipoth with female principle. While the Tree of Life represents light and masculine force of God, the Tree of Night is symbolic of darkness and female aspects, which in Qabalistic tradition are often viewed as evil and impure. They are emanations of Lilith, the Demon Goddess of Hebrew legends, who rules the realms of Qlipoth together with Samael or Lucifer. The offspring born from their unholy union is Beast 666, Chiva, the Antichrist, who rules the heart of the Tree—the solar sphere of Thagirion.

There are several initiatory models existing within the present Qlipothic magic. They are practiced by particular occult groups and they can also be learned by the practitioner alone, forming foundations for personal development. Tree of Qlipoth is one of these initiatory models. Qlipothic Initiation is based on 11 levels of the Tree of Night, which together constitute 11 initiatory steps. The first step is where the aspiring initiate begins the journey into the Nightside and it represents the opening of the Gates of the Soul for the energies of the Dark Tree. These initiatory levels bring the initiate to the heart of Darkness and transform man into God, as promised by the Serpent in Genesis 3:5, "Your eyes shall be opened, and ye shall be as gods, knowing good and evil." The last and eleventh step, which is taken on Thaumiel level, leads to the Void, beyond limits of the universe known to man.

Thaumiel Seal by edgar kerval

THIS IS A BRIEF OVERVIEW OF THE 11 LEVELS OF THE QLIPOTHIC PATH:

1. **LILITH (THE QUEEN OF THE NIGHT)** - The Gate to the Unknown. Here the initiate encounters first guides and allies on the path and here the consciousness opens for the contact with the Nightside. Lucifer's Ascending Flame is ignited and Lilith approaches to guide the initiate through the paths of the Dark Side. The Goddess of the first Qlipha is Naamah. She is the one who holds dominion over material things. She can bestow all material gifts on the magician but she is despotic and difficult to deal with. Naamah is Lilith's demonic sister and they often come together as first guides into the Nightside.

2. **GAMALIEL (THE OBSCENE ONE)** - The Astral Sphere of Dreams. Here the initiate explores mysteries of witchcraft and sexual alchemy. The Goddess of the Moon is encountered and She introduces the adept into

secrets of lunar magic. In the sphere of Gamaliel all forbidden fantasies, repressed lusts and dreams come to the light of consciousness. The Goddess of Gamaliel is Lilith, who appears as a beautiful woman with the body of the serpent. She seduces the magician and guides us through the dark side of our own instincts. She is the queen of demons, and together with Lucifer, she rules the whole Qlipothic Tree.

3. SAMAEL (POISON OF GOD) - The alchemical Poison is drunk and it works its way through the initiate's consciousness, facing the initiate with tests of insanity, doubt and disbelief. The contact with personal Shadow is made and it becomes the Reaper, teaching the initiate about mysteries of death and soul flight. Here, in the Desert of Adramelech, the adept is faced with the ordeal of faith and devotion. Adramelech is the ruler of this Qlipha and appears as half-human half-peacock. He endows the magician with pride and beauty, which, however, is illusory and is a part of his initiatory test.

4. A'ARAB ZARAQ (THE RAVEN OF DISPERSION) - Mysteries of Venus and Luciferian magic. The initiate enters the path of eroto-mysticism and ordeals of the warrior. A'arab Zaraq brings destruction of all order, often through war and strife, also through death. The ruling God of this Qlipha is Baal, the god of war. He appears as a warrior with a horned helmet and spear. He instructs the magician in the art of invisibility and teaches the meaning of Luciferian freedom. His consort and ruling Goddess of this sphere is Dark Venus, who reveals further mysteries of sexual magic.

5. THAGIRION (THE DISPUTER) - The Illumination of the Nightside with the Light of the Black Sun. The initiate experiences the union of God and Beast and learns the idea of Godhood. Thagirion is the sphere of the Daimon, personal image of Godhood, and the Beast 666, who continuously strives to take dominion over human instincts. The ruling God of this Qlipha is Belphegor, the Lord of the Dead. Originally, Belphegor was a Moabite deity named Baal-Peor, who appeared both as a male solar god and a female lunar goddess. Within works of magic, he manifests in his bestial form, but he also assumes the shape of a young woman. He endows the magician with wealth and imagination.

6. GOLACHAB (THE BURNING ONE) - The Apocalypse. The initiate becomes the Fire of Destruction. Through harsh sexual practices the initiate faces tests of lust and suffering. This is the Qlipha of fire—both the flame of creation and the blaze of destruction. The ruling God here is Asmodeus, who appears as a flaming, winged man. He represents both the force of fire and the power of sexuality, and incubi and succubi of this sphere are the strongest and the most violent of the whole Qlipothic Tree.

7. GHA'AGSHEBLAH (THE SMITER) - The other side of eroto-mysticism. Through ordeals of war and love the initiate becomes the Smiter. The energies of this Qlipha bring life or destruction. They destroy the substance of Creation which lies at the foundation of the universe. The ruling God here is Astaroth, the spirit with a poisoned breath, riding on the back of a dragon and holding a serpent in his hands. He sees through past, present and future. He is also the patron God of liberal arts.

8. SATARIEL (THE CONCEALER) - The opening of the Eye of Lucifer. The initiate faces tests of surrealism and absurdity and learns to find the Truth in what is concealed. Nothing here is as it seems. The ruling God of this Qlipha is Lucifuge—he who shuns the light. His descriptions appear in most of medieval and early-Renaissance grimoires and hierarchies of demons. He reveals hidden treasures, but he can also drive the magician to madness.

9. GHAGIEL (THE HINDERER) - The lightening of the Luciferian Star. The initiate breaks the Divine Law and prepares for entering the Throne of Lucifer. This is the Qlipha of breaking rules and shattering foundations of the world. The ruler of this sphere is Beelzebub, the Lord of Flies.

10. THAUMIEL (TWINS OF GOD) - The accomplishment of the Promise given by the Serpent. The initiate becomes God. This Qlipha is split in two and has two ruling Gods: Satan and Moloch. Thaumiel is the adversary of Kether. The energies of this sphere represent eternal movement, active timelessness. The original meaning of "Satan" is the Adversary. In the Old Testament he was the accuser and he tempted and tested the faith of humans by leading them astray. Moloch was a Canaanite god whose rites included sacrificing children by burning.

11. THAUMIEL - The Void. The initiate steps beyond the universe known to man, into the Womb of the Dragon.

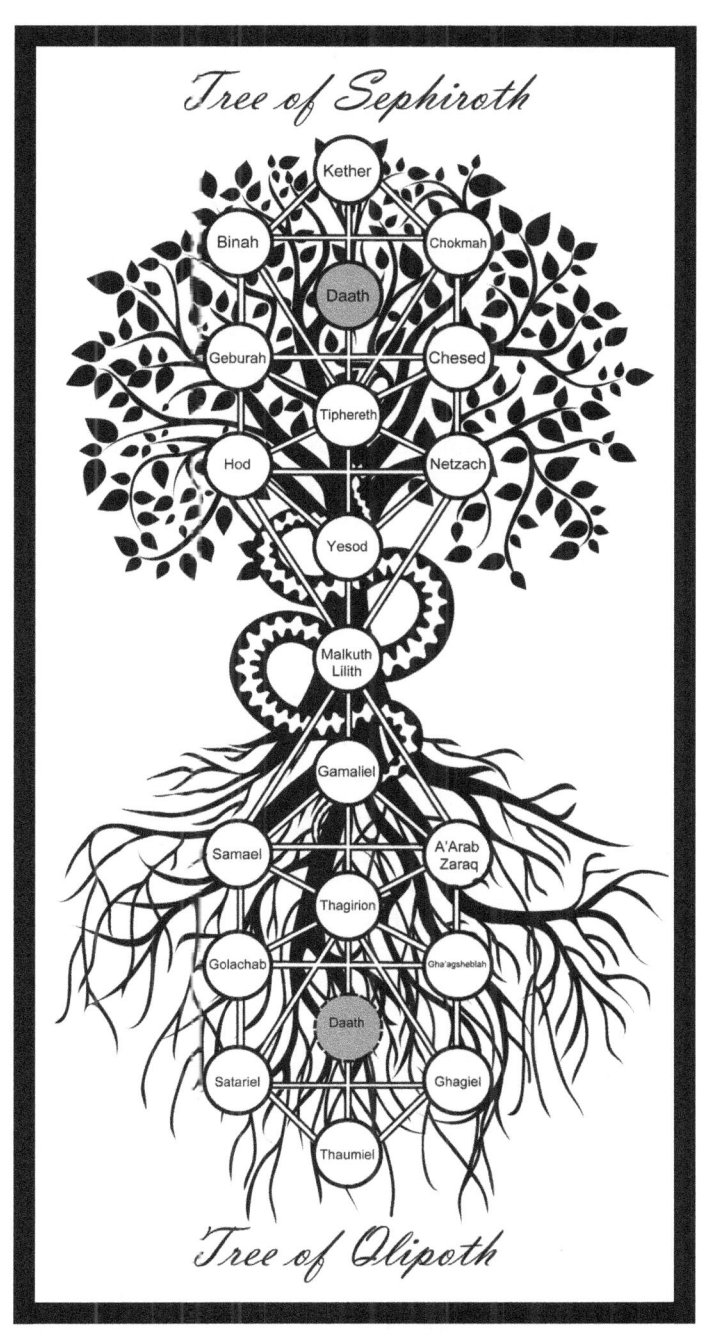

Qabalistic Tree by Aseanth Mason

Each Qlipha represents antithesis of the respective Sephirah. Qlipothic influence on the material world manifests in many different forms. This manifestation may be purely metaphysical, such as activity of demons, evil spirits, and other beings popularly associated with "the supernatural lore," but it can also manifest through physical phenomena, such as natural catastrophes, all sorts of accidents and misfortune, or normal, mundane problems. In traditional Qabalah, the gate to the Tree of Night is the hidden Sephirah Daath ("Knowledge"). It opens the way to the so-called Tunnels of Set that connect particular Qlipothic realms with one another, in a similar way as the Sephiroth are connected by pathways on the Tree of Life. However, Daath is not the only way to enter the realm of Qlipoth. Doorways to the Nightside are also found in the lowest world on the Qabalistic Tree, Malkuth/Lilith. Many Qabalists believed that the forces of Qlipoth belonged to this particular realm and were merely an extension of Malkuth. The Lilith Qlipha is described as a "cave," "crack," "cavern" in the earth through which man can enter the dark side of the Tree.

Working with the dark side of the Qabalah is a difficult and demanding task, but it is also a rewarding process which embraces and re-integrates each aspect of existence, opening access to the very source of primordial power. Tree of Qliphoth is a working initiatory model that leads to Self-Deification and empowerment. Particular Qlipothic realms can be viewed as actual worlds or as states of consciousness. You have to remember, however, that these are rather conceptions than actual structures, and what you see and experience in these spheres is a projection of your consciousness. Each initiatory level is different for each adept and there are never two identical forms of experience. The purpose of constructing such an initiatory model is to provide a system, or a "map," which will help the initiate progress through successive levels in a systematic way. Otherwise, we would lose ourselves in these dark and chaotic worlds. These realms have to be explored one by one and their powers gained successively.

For instance, if you choose to work with Thaumiel while you have just taken your initiation into Gamaliel, with your limited skills and your present level of magical development, you will only be able to experience a small percentage of the total power that awaits you on more advanced levels. It will be a mere glimpse into these realms and what they hold. If you approach them successively, according to a structured initiatory model, you will have access to all the power, and you will gain powerful allies among gods and

Qlipothic Initiation

spirits who manifest through these spheres. Besides, once you open your consciousness to the flow of energies from a particular Qlipothic level, this force will flow into your life whether you want it or not.

These doors cannot be closed. If your mind is not developed enough to withhold and harness these forces, they will only wreak havoc in your life and in the world around. There are many magicians whose worlds broke apart after they started working with the Qlipoth. Their family members died, their relationships broke, they lost their jobs and financial ability, their health deteriorated, and they were suddenly faced with more problems than they could ever imagine. If the left-hand-path initiation is taken step by step and approached with cautiousness and responsibility, it becomes the road to knowledge and power. Otherwise, it is a direct route to self-destruction.

Even if the meaning and nature of the initiatory process may seem abstract and incomprehensible at first, once you experience the whole thing, understanding will come in a natural and spontaneous way. All that was safe, familiar, or taken for granted is reversed and questioned. All that was a fantasy becomes real. The whole world is turned upside down. But what you see is a projection of your mind, the poison of the alchemical Dissolution working its way through your consciousness. If you succeed through this ordeal, you will be faced with alchemical Coagulation—you will find meaning in what you experienced, faith in disbelief, order in chaos, power in vulnerability. You will find your place in Infinity and Light in Darkness. The path that seemed to blur and disappear is now cleared and spreads far ahead. Inner emptiness is filled with wholeness. You will find new meaning in life and become reborn to the world. This makes initiation a beautiful and rewarding experience, if only you are open and ready to receive what it brings.

THE GRIMOIRE OF TIAMAT

By Asenath Mason

Out now via Nephilim Press

Tiamat Is The Primal Dragon Goddess, "the First One, who Gave Birth to the gods of the universe," the mother of everything, the self-procreating womb, the source of all life and all manifestation, the dragon of the void. Her gnosis is terrying, demanding and transformative on all possible levels of existence. It will take the practitioner to the very womb of chaos, where the soul will be devoured, dissolved, transformed, and reborn, in order to become the dragon essence, the living incarnation of this primordial current.

The work described in this book was inspired by the Babylonian epic known as the *Enuma Elish*, one of the oldest creation myths in the world. It contains methods and techniques to open the gateways to the Nightside and access the timeless essence of tiamat and 11 demon gods who were born in her black water of chaos. Rituals presented here constitute a framework for the application of gnosis that was revealed through the teachings of the demon-gods themselves and are laid down here specifically for those who seek self-deification in the modern world.

All rituals described in this book were performed and tested and their results have been verifed to prove their efficacy, both through self-initiatory work and through manifestation of their results on the physical plane. Therefore, they provide a solid ritual system which lays foundations for the further work with forgotten gnosis.

THE PATH OF NASA & ALCHEMICAL CATHARSIS

S. Connolly

Even within the primordial chaos the cyclic nature of all things rages unchecked. Both cruel and kind, life and death are the subtle transformations and regeneration of all things. Within this chaos is the divine intelligence. The Daemonic forces that rule over all things in creation, including those processes that manifest alchemical transformations. In these energies we find Daemons of dissolution, purification, distillation and even putrefaction. Of putrefaction there is Nasa, a Persian-based Daemonic force that rules over all dead matter. This is no small thing. Putrefaction is at work in our lives daily and we can learn a great deal from this process and its ruling Daemonic force, Nasa.

Putrefaction is a process of Saturn and sits beyond the abyss, on the pillar of severity in Binah. In this instance it is also a process that exerts itself most visibly on the material plane. Don't let this fool you. There is a great deal of both mental and spiritual change where putrefaction is at work.

In the past year, I donned my alchemist's cap and began growing mandragora officinalis. Mandrake is a Saturn herb and in Daemonolatry it is often used in ascension practice. That is, the practice of ascending to the Daemonic to partake of the wisdom that is divine intelligence. In this instance, the mandrake is taken internally. The leaves are cooling and are not nearly as toxic as the root. Ingesting it has the effect of giving the magician clarity of sight (both visual and empathic) and heightened intuition. Many people report feeling more present and describe their senses as being more vivid when ingesting mandrake tinctures or essences. Please note that this article is in no way suggesting you ingest poisonous plant matter, just pointing out that some people do so for the purposes outlined.

My purpose in sharing all of this will become rather apparent shortly. After growing the mandrake almost a year, I decided to begin tincturing the leaves. Clearly there are several methods to do this. One is to simply cut the fresh leaves from the plant and immerse them in alcohol (usually vodka or rum), or to remove fresh leaves, bruise and cut them, then immerse them into the alcohol. The other method is to create the tincture via a method of putrefaction. Putrefaction is one of those processes that a lot of magicians don't pay a lot of heed to unless they're fermenting their own home brew. Let's face it, most putrefaction stinks and most people would certainly not want to imbibe it in any shape or form. It was putrefaction that I chose as my method to tincture the mandrake and let me tell you why.

Putting a tincture through the putrefaction process reminds us that even from dead matter, something new is born. We encounter a great deal of dead matter in our lives whether we're clearing our gardens for winter, cleaning out the fridge, moving forward from a dead relationship, or moving on after a loved one dies. Dead matter is dead matter both figuratively and literally.

However, the mandrake leaves put through the putrefaction process don't start dead. Just as dead matters in our lives don't start out dead either. All these things begin as living, vibrant situations or matters with active energy flowing through them. It's when the leaves are cut from the living plant that the putrefaction process begins. Not all the leaves are cut, just one or two. The leaves are then added to distilled water and covered. There, within the darkness of the covered container, the plant matter begins to rot and decompose into the water, its essence absorbed, concentrated, into the water. As the weeks pass, a new leaf is added to the water and more water is added as needed. The plant matter goes from living to dead. This process is repeated for at least one moon cycle. At the completion of the process, all the plant matter has decayed into the water, and the now dead plant matter steeping in the water smells rather unpleasant. Putrid.

This is often how we find dead matter in our own lives. We tend to purposefully cut those living branches that no longer suit our purposes. Some wither, dry up and crumble on their own, but other situations are placed in water as if to preserve them, only for us to come back and discover the matter is most certainly dead and it smells rather unpleasant. However, from the death of a thing comes enlightenment about that thing. Hindsight is, after all, 20/20. This is where Binah, and understanding, in the nature of Saturn, comes in to play.

When you look at a dead situation with new eyes, it becomes apparent then that one can now filter out the dead matter while hanging onto the essence of what once existed as a vibrant, living thing. In the putrefaction experiment we simply bottle this essence. We filter the dead plant matter from the now foul-smelling water. The once clear water, even after having the matter filtered from it, has now turned a light hue of emerald green. An equal amount of clear alcohol, I prefer Vodka, is added to the liquid to tincture it. The putrid stench subsides and disappears. The essence of the plant is bottled.

In this, perhaps putrefaction is an exercise in letting go of the things that no longer serve us or help us grow. It's an exercise in moving forward and in understanding. These lessons may not always be kind as Saturn can be rather unkind in the lessons it teaches us.

We can still partake of the essence of what was, but in its new, alchemically transmuted form. While a mandrake tincture is taken three drops under the tongue at a time, enjoying a fleeting memory might suffice for our imbibement of our alchemically synthesized life experiences. Some may choose to purify the dead, but still solid, plant matter by submitting it to the fire. The ash can then be reincorporated into the tincture, or left as white ash (tangible salts), separated. This choice, like every decision we make to leave some things in our past or to carry them with us, is up to each individual.

It is in this we learn the wisdom of Nasa and partake of her. Dead matter(s) should be left to lie fallow. From them comes rebirth from the essence of what once was. In studying putrefaction we are actually studying the process of regeneration.

When my putrefaction experiment was done, my mandrake suddenly began to turn yellow. The leaves withered and died, and I was left with a pot containing a root. I patiently watered the barren pot for a month, allowing him to lay fallow, when after a month I noticed green shoots rising again from the soil. The mandrake itself does not teach putrefaction but rather another process of regeneration and the purpose of patience, the purpose of Saturn, the taskmaster planet. Think of Saturn as a strict professor who demands excellence from his students and you'll understand why processes, plants, and even the Qliphothic sphere ruled by this planetary body sit on the pillar of severity and force patience, work and processes like putrefaction. Ultimately these things make us stronger, wiser, bolder, and more prepared to face life's many challenges.

If you are not an alchemist or simply have no patience to grow a mandrake and prepare a tincture via the putrefaction process, there are other ways to harness the power of this process. That is to work directly with the Daemon, Nasa. The following ritual can be performed to share in her understanding and the process of leaving behind that which no longer serves you. It is a ritual of putrefaction that will make evident the things that must be left behind, while helping you synthesize and separate the useful essences of the experience.

On a Saturday, on a square of parchment, a piece of wood, or a piece of clay—draw the seal of Nasa. You can heed the planetary hour as well if you so choose.

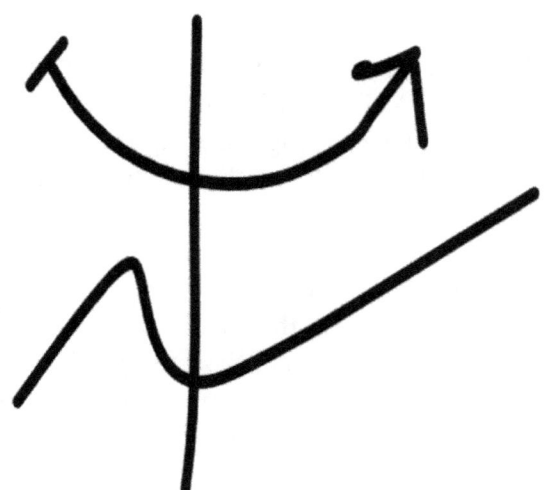

nasa putrefaction by S. connolly

The Path of Nasa & Alchemical Catharsis

Notice the alchemical symbolism contained within the sigil itself. On the opposite side of the seal, draw the fourth pentacle of Saturn. This will draw the planetary influence into the talisman.

saturn4 by S.connolly

Carry this with you for one week, in your left pocket for men, or at your left breast for women. If you would like to skip this step, simply feed the talisman a drop of your blood.

Also on a Saturday, open your temple to perform your ritual (based on your preferences), invoking any Daemons or spirits you see fit for The Work, along with Nasa using her Enn:

Akayma eya ana ta Nasa

The serpent wise deals death to lies. Remember this as the end falls from your lips, its ending hissed. Now, holding the talisman in your hands, visualize the process of putrefaction. A plant decaying in water. Flesh decaying and dissolving. Consequently there are many choices among the death daemonic that would also be suited to this task or would work well paired with

Nasa. Now imagine all of these images and thoughts filling the talisman. Close your ritual as you normally would and take your talisman to your bed. Place the talisman beneath your bed for a week. During this time, dreams and revelations of those things no longer useful to you will surface and the useful essence will become apparent.

You may also choose to carry the talisman with you. Again, for men in the left pocket, for women at the left breast, but be careful as this may cause more abrupt endings or will serve to sever ties more readily. To put it bluntly, relationships could abruptly end, people could die. Projects can falter. The talisman can be kept wrapped in black cloth in a wooden or clay container, recharged, and reused as you need it, or you may give it back to the earth or the flame so that its power will naturally dissipate and go back to all that is.

Ultimately the Path of Nasa, the path of putrefaction, can be the catalyst for a cathartic event that will bring you rebirth and renewal. Never look upon the death of a thing as a closed door. END.

Another Round by Isabele Gaborit

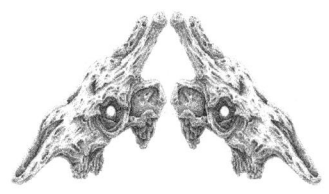

Unguentum Sabbati

Matthew Venus

In locked retreat of temple room,
I wait, alone in twilight's gloom.
To break free from the earthly tomb,
As night's departing rite doth loom.

In hidden realm waits silently
My lover, guised in misery.
In twisted veil of grotesque form,
And beauty kin to tempest storm.

A vessel housed in blessed cask,
On hallowed nights he howls his psalm.
Wearing deceitful trickster's mask,
And blesses with his baneful balm.

I stand before him, celebrant,
Awaiting twelfth strokes chime,

Qliphoth Opus III

When low groan turns to fevered chant,
And shadows step in-time.

The sprites and imps come out from cold,
Then strip me to the skin.
They whisper words arcane and old,
And signal to begin.

With pinch and scratch they redden me,
Preparing flesh for our esprit,
As I call forth the Noctifer,
and smoke rises from smoldering myrrh.

Then by a sweet venefic touch,
caressed upon my form.
He holds desire by poisoned clutch,
And sets free midnight's swarm.

I draw him into every pore,
to bear the mark of Cain.
His hands anoint and then explore,
Both sacred and profane.

I don his boon as witches clothes,
And dance to tune sung out by crows.
A dark arrangement by Old Nick;
The Hallowing of Heretic.

The Corvids sing the blackest song,
In Caws and Croaks I sing along,
And hear by ear of twisted tree,
The midnight song they sing to me.

"Thout, tout a tout tout,
Throughout and about, about!
Feral child of eyeless sight,
come to join us in our flight!

Unguentum Sabbati

"Be Hallowed now in bone and skin,
Hallowed as our rites begin,
Hallowed as your darkest twin,
Hallowed now go forth to Him!"

And by their voice the ground is loosed,
My senses frayed upon their mesh.
My very soul becomes seduced,
And casts off fetters of the flesh.

By besom, stang, and nightmare's horse,
My baleful brethren stride.
While I upon the serpent's back,
To Darkest Mass shall ride.

They come by hopping of the toad,
And by the swift-foot hare.
We wind about the crooked road,
Until we all meet there.

Arrived upon the blasted spot,
A crossed roads church, the Devils Plot.
Where foolish souls are sold and bought,
Yet stands the forge where wisdom's wrought.

And while preparing to begin,
We reunite with witching kin.
Regale with tales of where we've been,
On nights when clothed in other skin.

When come arrived by spirit track,
The shades of those once gone, come back.
The blessed dead to join our rite,
Awakened now from grave's respite.
Ancestral revenants process, led
By cavalcade of Mighty Dead.

Qliphoth Opus III

The ancient kings of ancient thrones,
step light to song of rattled bones.

Next darkness becomes lit aflame,
By blessed ones of speechless name,
Of ageless power left untamed,
Led by their beauteous, fearsome Dame,
Their place of honor come to claim,
The goodly ones of all Elphame.

The moon rides high, the crowd doth grow,
In Devil's darkest field fallow.
Then by the sounding of horns blow,
And heralded by groaning woe,
Our dance begins, and as we go,
We circle round and step in tow,
To dirgesome song from bleak bellow,
lit by hag's tapers sorcerous glow.
The power play of ebb and flow,
With treading steps grinding and slow,
Where dragging heel begins to hoe,
A trough made as ploughman's furrow.
Within which, baneful seeds we sow.
By shuffled wailing to and fro,
In echo of taboo tableau,
We call our lord up from below.

We conjure him from lands remote,
Out from bramble and briar.
A charm called out from book unwrote,
And sung by Sabbath's Choir.
A grim decry from guttural throat,
And cause for Papal ire.
We sing to him, the Witches Goat,
Our Magister and Sire.

Unguentum Sabbati

While smoke rises, up from balefire,
And flames stand as infernal spire,
Our voices call out ever higher,
Toward ecstasies which we aspire.
Then manifest by our desire,
To bless and blight as we require,
Our Lord, invoked by Mass entire,
Comes bounding forth from lighted pyre.

He rests himself on grandest throne,
In circle marked by standing stone.
While silence falls on woeful groan,
and senses become overthrown,
The wildwood's musk, our Lords cologne,
Entices each, from lad to crone.

New prospects clamber to be sworn,
And have signature took,
With blood drawn out by prick of thorn,
and stamped in Black Bound Book.

His servants list off the devout,
Announcing loud each name,
And swiftly spin them round about,
To grant the kiss of shame.

Then all adjourn to table made,
For Sabbath's furious feast,
With delicacies laid and splayed,
Fore ravenous man and beast.

One to one we fill each seat,
And savor every bite,
Of banquets bounties sour and sweet,
Which arouse and excite.

Qliphoth Opus III

On my left hand and to my right,
Faithful familiars sit.
While cross from me in feasts twilight,
Imps suckle witches tit.

We carry on, carouse and eat,
Unceasing through the night.
Until we're sated and replete,
Each daemon, witch, and wight.

And then a new psalm we intone,
While circling bout the place we've flown.
Which leads by pounding visceral drone,
Our Feast of Flesh. A fierce cyclone,
Where panting escalates to moan,
All heights and depths are bared and shown.
The Children of WitchBlood and bone,
Writhe naked bout a great hagstone.
A pleasure dance beyond atone;
and orgy of the Devil's own.

Then from his throne he fixes me,
His monstrous child and devotee,
In wildest throes of revelry,
Whilst my familiars writhe with me.
Our savage rites turning the key,
To highest realms of ecstasy.

He seizes me amongst the flock,
His gaze ensnares me, fiery eyed.
Raw inhibition now defrocked,
And I stand naked by his side.

A lustful beast from cage unlocked,
I climb his frame and sit astride.
Ensorcelled by his glorious cock,
Benison bursting forth inside.

Unguentum Sabbati

He feasts on me, the Lord Twice-Born,
And fevered frenzy reaches height.

While fire blazes twixt blackest horns;
The dawn's light breaks through dark of night.

Without so much as wink or warn,
Rentum Tormentun lays it's blight.
From Hexentanz we all are torn,
And cast away in mournful flight.

By rushing voices sounding boom,
The winding winds lift up and churn.
Upon the gales by stang and broom,
The faithful ones swiftly return.

And I awake, in temple room,
Solemn, in first morn's light.
The fettered flesh, mine to resume,
Until next Sabbath's night.

Baphometis by Matthew Venus

Qalilitu:
The Evil Mermaid From The Bloody Water Of Gamaliel

Daemon Barzai

Qalilitu is an evil mermaid that dwells deep into Gamaliel's bloody lakes. She appears as half-woman, half-fish. Her eyes are completely white, and she has a fiery third eye on her forehead. She has wild reddish hair and very sharp teeth. It's very frequent to have visions about underwater temples, filled with skulls and bones that belonged to her previous victims. She is an evil seductress. She doesn't speak, but instead she is able to communicate telepathically. She is a shape-shifting vampire spirit that can teach us how to devour our victims on the astral plane. She is always bloodthirsty and enjoys blood sacrifices.

There are different ways to work with this spirit. One of them is to evoke her through a water medium, like a black bowl filled with water. When we invoke her, she will change our astral body and we'll have the skill of shape-shifting. In this new form we'll be able to hunt on the astral plane. Also, we can invoke her in a maledicted work, in which case she will drain the vital energy off the victim, and this is a powerful black magic ritual. In exchange, she will require a sacrifice which could be either an astral sacrifice or a blood sacrifice.

Finally, we can use pathworking or dream working to get in contact with her.

The Bloody Underwater Temple

- Pathworking -

Relax both mind and body, close your eyes and when you feel ready, begin with the following visualization:

You are at a sea shore, the full moon illuminates the place, and from the water you hear a sound, a scream. Follow the sound. You are inside the water, and an unknown force sucks you into the water. Everything around you is dark, and you cannot see anything. Follow the sound. You go deeper and deeper and you see a red light. Go there. You cross the light and you are in a temple with four black columns and on the floor you can see thousands of skulls and bones. Whisper the name *"Qalili.tu"*. She appears in front of you. She is majestic, sensual, seductress and evil. She is half-woman, half-fish. She has red hair, white eyes and a fiery third eye on her forehead. She shows you an altar of sacrifices. Talk to her and ask about her powers and skills. Do not force anything; let the rest of the vision come in a natural way.

When you are ready to finish the experience, just come back to your normal state of consciousness. You can continue working with this in your dreams.

The Invocation of Qalilitu

Light some suitable incense, e.g., Musk or Sandalwood. Light black candles and drop some of your blood on the seal below, when you are ready, begin with the invocation:

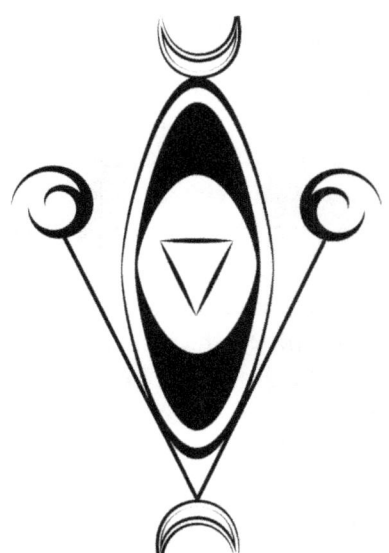

Qalilitu Seal by Daemon Barzai

QALILITU

Melez!

Qalilitu, Evil Mermaid

Come from the Bloody Waters on Gamaliel!

In the name of Lilith,

Queen of Hell

Mistress of Vampires!

Come!

Teach me your secrets!

Bloody Creature that dwells on the deeps of Gamaliel's Waters!

Come to this flesh temple!

I invoke you seductress Spirit!

You seduce your victim with your songs

And with your hellish beauty!

And then you devour its souls!

Evil spirit from the Black Waters!

Come to my temple!

In the name of the Dragon!

So mote it be!

Ho Drakon Ho Megas!

BECOMING HOODOO
PART 3

Kyle Fite

In the Microcosmic Occult Occident, Voodoo is Funk, Cool as Shit and worth a High Five of Skin-Slapping "Can you hear it" Spirit. But it also grinds, crushes and humbles. If you wear the Light and Darkness as more than a fashion statement, it seeps into your pores and makes of them Tunnels through which the Christ descends into Hell to lead Captivity Captive. Voodoo will reveal the Deeper Mystery of Erzulie's Tears and show them as Stars.

Voodoo is, in fact, that Divine Light punching out a lens in your sunglasses as it brings us to Itself!

Now, when I think of the word HOODOO, I do not turn to what many call "Rootwork." I don't envision lines of brickdust or nails driven in the corners of a room. I don't think of "secret ingredients" casseroled to gastronomically guide the affections of a potential lover.

For myself, the word HOODOO conjures a vivid recollection of the first lesson in Michael Bertiaux's Grimoire *Lucky Hoodoo*. It was in these few pages that I was introduced to the Denizens of the Deadworld and their

Compatriots, the Transmigrated Atlantean Magi. This Strange Company led me to their Leaders who are nothing less than LWA. These two particular LWA (Papa Ghuedhe and Grand Bois) introduced me to the vast spectrum in which they move and have their Being. I was brought into their sacred space, removed from my body and lifted up into the "Seventh Heaven" as my Spirit-Self. What I saw below me was that which St. Paul considered unlawful to speak of. At the center of a vast and scintillating cosmic web sat a Spider God, enthroned upon the entire matrix of Being. Within this Spider God was a Cross and upon this Cross was nailed a figure called Luage. I saw that the Cross was also a Living Being and its Name was Legbha. And these two became ONE. As this happened, I was drawn into their midst and understood the mystery of the Blood and Water which flowed from the side of Christ.

The Spider God moved as Lightning and I became a Lightning Rod, a ROOD poised for Union with the Rose of Time. I felt flexion of the Divine Yoni beyond all flesh and wept at the Grace. All of this came down into my Body as Tongues of Fire and I rose from the Dead as Zombi.

My Urthself was then beheld as Gameself. Kyle, the Earthman, woke to see this vision retreating toward the Horizon. We forget our Dreams just as swiftly as our Oneiric Mindself forgets the Bodily Life.

The Hoodoo Pilot, however, chased these Spectres even as they chased the Setting Sun! The lens left in the frame then revealed its purpose. My Vision vaulted into a Sea of Seeing, black waves passing like stormclouds over the Sun. What we think of occluded consciousness is, in fact, an Action Field for the Gnostic Mind. The hoodwinked "Thinker" cannot rationalize his way into this Awareness. In fact, all rationale chases after the resonance found in creative expression of this Truth. It is the Gnostic Mind which is able to truly SEE the so-called "Illusory World," using its Modus Operandi to progressive effect. Light enters one eye and emanates from the other. Darkness is illumined until we understand that it was never really there.

HOODOO (Initiated Tech) is a Gate to VOODOO (SPIRIT) and VOODOO reifies in HOODOO.

VOODOO-HOODOO is, ultimately, SHIVA-SHAKTI. In this Divine Coupling, we may also understand the Mystery of Legbha-Luage.

Gran Bwa by kyle fite

We are Voyaging Hearts entering this Mystery that we may know OURSELVES both within and AS it!

X
Hoodoo Initiation Ritual

In the *Lucky Hoodoo* Grimoire, there is given a Ritual to perform whereby the Aspirant may contact the Hoodoo Spirits. It is a simple rite and requires very little beyond a sincere spirit and an open heart. Compared to the complexities of the Western Magical Tradition, this working may seem overly simplistic. It is my contention, however, that it can be accomplished through even MORE simple means.

Acquire a BLACK CANDLE.

Carve a CROSS into this Candle.

Light the Candle in a darkened room where it shall serve as the only light. KNOW that in the doing so, you are calling upon the Hoodoo Spirits.

This fusion of Light and Darkness, of Phallus (Candle) and Yoni (Surrounding Space), will surely bring forth Emissaries of the Two Great Loa. The Dark and Hard Earthstone of the Northern Cross will surely join with the Moist and Fertile Gateway in the West.

Stand with your arms outspread! Welcome these Emissaries in your own words. Welcome them with more than words! Welcome them with the Atomic and Sub-Atomic Substance of your Living Body!

The Bonelord will touch your marrow, infusing it with Ice and Fire. These elements will hiss and steam. As they join and liquefy, the Great Sunken City of Vilokan will rise to the surface. H.P. Lovecraft described this event in his classic tale, DAGON. Those who dread the unknown and its intrusion into status quo consciousness may find this happening as disturbing as the protagonist of that story. Those who welcome the inevitable trajectory of their human existence will find in this "Beauty From Hell."

When you extinguish this candle, know that it lights a wick within your Deepcore, illuminating the vast intelligence operating through the "Shadow Stuff" around you. This is a form of ectoplasm which now undulates over the surface of your skin, finding ingress through pores and orifices.

Goodnight. Tomorrow you wake into a Different Dimension.

Tomorrow you WAKE!

Hoodoo entry point by kyle fite

X
THE WORD OF HOODOO:

TRANSMIGRATION!

This Word is the Key to all Hoodoo Tech.

We'd lie if we said there wasn't power in our straw dolls, in our candle-work, herbalism and ritual action. The Hoodoo Man is rightly regarded when he operates in polaroids, matchsticks and figures formed of clay. But it must be emphasized that this is NOT because a recipe rightly followed doles out the dish.

The Hoodoo Man is a *Quantum Wizard*. He is not someone simply manipulating the minds of the Superstitious. Between the folklore and effect is a LINK and the Hoodoo Man exists within that Linkspace. This space is not easily entered. To come here, the Hoodoo Man had to become Voodoo Man. This meant a Sacrifice. Odin on the World Tree was Exemplar of this Giving. Young Ones filled with Piss, Vinegar and Hubris see "Wotan" as some Heroic Ideal. The "Gar" which wounded Odin, however, cut more than skin. It pierced every strata of experience and from this opening sprung lava. The lava consumed the flesh and the bones fell unto Earth.

There is an infinitude of difference between the skull sewn on your leather jacket and that which molders in your casket.

The latter is the wiser. Ask your Ancestors. They won't answer with Tongues of Clay.

X

So there I was, enjoying a nice quiet dissolution well beneath the surface world and its merry-go-round of pleasure and suffering.

Quite suddenly, there's a rap on my coffin and it opens with a creak.

"Hello, Kyle."

It's my Pals from Purgatory, of course.

I'm yanked out by bony fingers and someone shoves a cigar in my face.

"Hot time in the Old Town Tonight!"

Slapped, pushed, grabbed and groped, I dance a karmic kaleidoscope to a booze bent table in what I can only presume is some Pub in Hell. The cards are on the table and they're not playing Poker.

My Pals: "Deal."

Me: "What?"

Becoming Hoodoo Part 3

P: "What's the DEAL with you?"
M: "I'm not sure, I…"
P: " 'I, I, I..!' I-DEAL! So, what's it gonna be?"

Candles light themselves on the table, burn down and vanish in seconds. It's quite impressive, actually.

P: "Chickadee, gimmee your compact!"

The camera tilts and between perfect brown skin and the billowing frills of a pink cotton dress sewn in the early 1700's, tears float, anti-grav and anti-GRAVE. Through red-lipsticked laughter, a mirror is held in front of me like a winning hand.

I see in its surface a skull with two front teeth missing and something that looks like gang graffiti painted on the forehead.

Just then, the tip of a giant spade comes crashing through the plaster ceiling. My companions shriek and scuttle from the raining dust. Above me, two young men are chattering in a language I don't know. There's a sick popping beneath my chin and I've clearly been decapitated.

I get to travel in the comfort of a burlap bag to some shithole woodbox in South America. The charade in front of me evokes a longing for prime time TV. There's blood and sex and a chicken, cell phones snapping the spectacle, noxious smoke curling in the air. If I had arms and legs, I'd kick some ass (or at least make a yeoman's effort) but those parts were uncalled ceremoniously left behind.

As it goes, I catch my reflection in the scummed-up window I'm facing. There it is, that symbol on my forehead. The fog clears and the image pixelates. Coming into sharper view, the gangland graffiti on my grinning grimace is seen to be a single word:

DEMO.

The Brazilians heave my head back into the bag and retrace their path to my grave.

Upon arrival, they shake it out and begin shoveling soil over me until I can feel the weight of earth pushing me down into some chthonic undercurrent.

"Dispel Entropic Miasma, Okay? Deadlock Escape Mode: Operational!"

The Voice is familiar. I am not remembering with this Brain—nor with this Mind.

He is Here in the Nowhere, at the End where All Things Become.

The Doctor.

Baptism by Kyle fite

I approach a Lighthouse and enter, climbing its seven stories. In the uppermost chamber is a serpent coiled into the figure Eight, the Black Snake.

"Darkness Encircles Meonic Occupations."

Thin metal ladder to the top.

"Durtal Evolves! My Otherness!"

Kammamori smiles.

"The Doctor is in," I say.

"Yes," he replies. "But what man at ease would seek him? GET OUT."

The Light becomes a Furnace and I am engulfed in flames. I am the Candle Wick seen through Brazilian eyes as it throws off Yellow, Blue, Green and Red. Blood rushes back into the chicken's neck as it crawls into its own egg. Shiva-Shakti radiate from the Heart of Dainichi Nyorai. Lam's latex head falls forward and bubbles on the candle's flame. Doctor Kammamori is Fu Manchu and Damns Every Movement Otherwise.

"HOODOO," he says, "operates between Being and its BECOMING. The Grand BECOMING which followed the Atlantean Deluge entailed an encoding of Intentional Form in a Quantum Plasma which could both survive and re-enter what we regard as Terrestrial Spacetime. We speak of the Deluge as if it occurred in the past but this is due to the limits of your language."

I venture to state my understanding.

"This is because there is only the NOW, is that right?"

"It is true that there is no Past or Future—but there is also NO NOW. Through understanding the latter point, we may enter the 8-fold Spider Space of Time and impress its Webwork with our Will. Crowley made a big deal of his formula Love Under Will. But—what is WILL under?"

I open my mouth to answer, but before I can speak, the Doctor places a small capsule on my tongue.

"Rx…SILENCE."

Dharmakara by kyle fite

The Serpent's Servants: Disciples of Ain

Matthew Wightman

Impossibility. A mundane word to some. Difficult to truly imagine in a world where it is often said that anything and everything is possible even if improbable. We get a glimpse of impossibility when we attempt to imagine True Impossibility, the fundamental impossibility of all possibilities. Our imagination comes up against impossibility in this moment and finds that it is indeed impossible to imagine that which cannot be imagined, for imagination is itself founded upon possibility. Nevertheless, True Impossibility was one of the infinite possibilities within the Void that was beyond all distinction including that between possibility and impossibility—the Void from which the Ain Sof emerged. I call this True Impossibility, Ain.

In the beginning, before words such as 'beginning' had any meaning, there was the Void of distinction. This was the ultimate regression of transcendence, beyond possibility and impossibility, beyond being and non-being, beyond emptiness and fullness. As part of that fullness emerged two desires: one for possibility and the other for impossibility, the fulfillment of either of which would eliminate the Void. The two co-existed in perfect balance; however, the desire for possibility feared its sibling. It became possessed by A(i)nxiety that the other desire would manifest itself first and all would be lost permanently. Driven mad by this A(i)nxiety, the desire for possibility manifested itself in such a way that it contained the other desire within itself so that it could thereby be controlled. Thus, the Ain Sof was born.

With the manifestation of the Ain Sof, the Void of distinction was annihilated, replaced by the actuality of the Ain Sof who was in all respects identical to the Void from which it emerged, entirely without distinction, except for the fact that it had chosen possibility over impossibility and therefore contained a single distinction. The Ain Sof was to become the actualized possibility of the True God beyond-being; God beyond God for whom the name God is diminutive. The Ain Sof is the matrix of all possibilities and of all possible relations. It is the limitless depths of the Void, absolutely unconditioned and simple. Yet it is beyond unity and multiplicity. The Ain Sof is simultaneously without multiplicity or complexity and yet infinitely complex and multiple (or at least the ground of possibility for such complexity) without destroying its simple unity. 'Infinity' is insufficient to describe it as it also contains the possibility for finitude. In its infinity the Ain Sof also contains Ain, the possibility of no possibilities. No creation, no God, no nothing. This is the ultimate oblivion beyond oblivion: the Oblivion of Oblivions.

From within the infinity of the Ain Sof emerged a further desire possessed by its own A(i)nxiety caused by the continued presence of Ain within the Ain Sof. This desire distinguished itself further by emanating as the Ain Sof Aur in an attempt to make more permanent the divine reality. This is the intentionality of God, the aspect of God that chooses from the limitless possibilities to form Godself beyond-being. This is the God we come to know and the only God able to be known. It is the Tetragrammaton; the invisible expression of the Sefirot that is expressed in and by creation; the Beatific Vision; the Shekhinah; the invisible Torah.

The Ain Sof Aur, driven by both Love and A(i)nxiety, originated creation in its pure timeline for the purpose of finding expression for its limitless Love and to make permanent the choice for possibility in being without itself becoming. Desiring a lover capable of such expression, the Ain Sof Aur distinguished itself from that which it is not—non-being/being—desiring that it becomes. From this desire emerged a second beyond-being, the Sefirot, entirely independent from the first and in all respects alike except that it was united with being. This creation was to be the perfect reflection of the Ain Sof Aur in every way. Unbeknownst to the Ain Sof Aur, this also meant that not only would its A(i)nxiety manifest in creation but the latent desire for Ain contained within the Ain Sof and Ain Sof Aur would be made manifest as well.

Enter, Lilith and Samael. Lilith, as the first woman, was meant to be Adam's perfect soul-mate who would flawlessly reflect the Love of the Ain Sof Aur. However, little did the Ain Sof Aur realize that Lilith's desire was not for creation but for anti-cosmic Oblivion. She fled Eden and there She met Samael, her true soul-mate, chief among the Ain Sof Aur's Angelic Host who had strayed from his designated role to pursue His own anti-cosmic agenda. Samael, like the human Lilith, was intended to be a pure reflection of the Love of God. Blinded by its A(i)nxiety, however, the Ain Sof Aur failed to notice that Samael's true loyalties lay not with the Ain Sof Aur but with Ain. When Samael and Lilith united their mutual desire for Ain, it manifested itself in the Nachash, the Serpent. The Serpent was the ultimate agent of Ain, the anti-cosmic Messiah (anointed One) of Oblivion. Together, Samaelilith is the true manifestation of the desire for Ain that the Ain Sof feared within the Void.

The Serpent, completely free of A(i)nxiety, was the most cunning of all creatures and was a master of exploiting the weaknesses of others. It saw the A(i)nxiety of creation and used it to tempt creation away from the loving purposes of the Ain Sof Aur, knowing that such an act would lead to the eventual insanity and fracturing of the divine reality, which would in turn lead both God and creation down the road toward Ain. To the Ain Sof Aur's horror, creation turned on its creator out of A(i)nxiety caused by its own capacity to choose Ain, slothfully capitulating its existence beyond-being to dwell in the banal safety of the lifeless clay of being. The externalized beyond-being then became an object of worship—the Demiurge.

If the Serpent is completely free of A(i)nxiety, the Demiurge is completely possessed by it. Obsessed with its continued existence, the Demiurge will stop at nothing to ensure the perpetuation of Being and the clayborn's externalization of their beyond-being. This reality is magnified exponentially when the Ain Sof Aur—who put its hope in the capacity of its children to follow the Beatific Vision back to it as if they had not strayed—goes insane and attempts to overcome creation in its wayward Messiah, Jesus Christ, only to be overcome by Christ and made one with the Demiurge. The Ain Sof Aur thereby becomes God the Father who closes the womb of non-being from which creation originally emerged. As such, the Demiurge is a bloated monstrosity sustaining creation in its suffering simply for the sake of continuing to be.

(1) We cannot see past that which we fear. As Frank Herbert aptly put it, "Fear is the mind-killer" (Dune, 1965).

The insanity of the Ain Sof Aur, which issued suffering into the divine reality, threatened to destabilize the Ain Sof. From this suffering arose the Ain Sof Choshek; the lamenting God of limitless darkness; our Dark Mother Tanninim; the Nightside Tetragrammaton and the last surviving personhood of the divine. The Ain Sof Choshek is the last bastion of the original True God, the Ain Sof. It survives insanity by inhabiting lament and grief and thereby paradoxically maintains the integrity of the Ain Sof. Like the Serpent, its desire is for Ain, for an end to suffering both created and divine. Like the Ain Sof Aur before it, the Ain Sof Choshek undergoes tzimtzum, creating a womb of non-being from which a new beyond-being, the Klifot of the Sitra Achra, emanates. Just as the insanity of the Ain Sof Aur is an event beyond time, so too does the splitting of the divine desire, which gives rise to the Ain Sof Choshek, have eternal reverberations. The emanation of the Klifot causes a recreation whereby all being receives a parasitic Shadow that seeks to diminish the being of the host. In this alternate timeline, Tanninim exists before the act of creation responding in wrath against the Ain Sof Aur's violent creative act, knowing that it will result in the Great Nightmare of Being. Yahweh the Demiurge attempts to subdue Tanninim by objectifying the Tehom and claiming to have created the Tanninim on the fifth day. This act adds great insult to reprehensible injury.

The insanity of the Ain Sof Aur brought on by Jesus' defection to the Demiurge (the externalized and divinized Sefirot) happens beyond time, and thus is neither temporal nor historical. Therefore, when the Ain Sof Aur responds to Jesus' abandonment—a linear temporal-historical event—pouring itself into creation—both an eternal and historical event—the act has reverberations throughout history, extending from beginning to end. Just as John rewrites Genesis, Christ rewrites creation, creating it in his image. Christ truly is at the beginning and the world is created for Christ just as Christians claim. The Ain Sof Aur accomplishes this creation by raping Tanninim and using her womb, the last source of non-being—the Tehom—to bring forth his bastard creation. Thus, the Demiurge becomes the Original Rapist, the Original Evil, and Tanninim the Original Victim (a role Christ attempts to usurp).

The Serpent's Servants: Disciples of Ain

(2) Note that in my previous theological articles I refer to Tanninim as Tiamat. Through much reflection on this name and conversations with the Temple of the Black Light, I have decided that Tanninim is a more appropriate choice. Although this name is plural, referring to a collective rather than an individual, I see Tanninim as similar to Elohim when used to reference the Demiurge. Though not a proper name like Tiamat, it does have the advantage of encompassing the energies of the other primordial dragons, including Rahab, Leviathan, Yamm and the older dragons in whom they have their beginnings: Apsu, Mummu, and Kingu. As such, it is beyond the binary of male and female, yet retains the closeness to Motherhood in the womb of Chaos. Best of all it remains within the Klifotic/Hebraic mythos.

(3) Rather than a contraction of space, which as a dimension of being is not part of God's actuality, it is a distinction of non-being/being and beyond-being. God determines Godself as beyond-being and creation (in this case, the Klifot) as non-being desired to become in being (in the case of the Klifot, this desire is temporary until all Being has been eliminated). From this desire emerges a new beyond-being, the Sefirot and Klifot.

Worse still, Yahweh also claims to have crushed their heads—Psalm 74:13.

In this recreated timeline, Samael and Lilith exist as 'fallen' creatures and part of the Sitra Achra, manipulating reality from the Other Side. As such, the Serpent acts as an agent of the Ain Sof Choshek, whose desire is to end suffering through the choosing of Ain. While the Ain Sof Choshek is an agent of Ain due to the suffering and madness within the Godhead, the Serpent as the created embodiment of the desire for Ain is in reality prior to the Ain Sof Choshek's actuality, as the Serpent exists as the same entity in both the pure and recreated timelines. Unlike the Ain Sof Choshek, the Serpent desires Ain for its own sake. The Serpent, who is the first and the last, is able to intertwine and connect the trees of life and death from the central Sefirah/Klifah of Da'ath. The Serpent is able to unite fate with freedom, causality with acausality, being with beyond-being, just as God intended. It is into the Serpent's mouth that the fruit of life is devoured and out of which gnosis is given. The Serpent (and the fireborn who follow him/her) will both unite and bring an end to the Sefirot and Klifot by eating its own tail, returning all to non-being.

Having succeeded in manipulating God into desiring Ain, Samael and Lilith turned their sights on creation, hoping to awaken it to the horror of its existence within the Demiurge's false paradise. The Klifotic Fruit of Knowledge was meant to reveal the fundamental violence and suffering upon which existence is founded, opening the hearts and minds of creation to turn on the creator. Those who accept this knowledge, those whose inner Black Flame burns brightly, walk the Serpent's Path and are called fireborn.

It is this path of the Nachash that we, as the bearers of the Serpent's Seed, must follow. Qayin, born of the Nachash and Eve, possesses both the drive toward Ain and A(i)nxiety. Qayin, however, is the first human to accept his A(i)nxiety and set it aside. Creation could have similarly refused to be a victim of its own fear—just as the Ain Sof could have—and instead expressed only the Love of the Ain Sof Aur confining the drive to Ain within the Nachash. Only creation failed, capitulating itself to the manifestation and the embodiment of its fears, the Demiurge. This yielded suffering and violence within the created and divine realities, causing the Ain Sof Aur to go insane and the Ain Sof Choshek to arise from within the Ain Sof. All of this was foreseen and set into motion by the machinations of the Serpent. As children of the Black Light, the fireborn lineage of Qayin, we possess the spiritual Seed of the Serpent, the drive toward Ain. As the children of Eve we also possess A(i)nxiety. We are called upon to embrace our desire toward Ain and accept our A(i)nxiety while setting it aside just as Qayin did and as creation should have done at the beginning.

Many who call themselves anti-cosmic Satanists seek to return to the chaotic womb of Tanninim where the Demiurgic Law binding being to fate and causality is non-existent. There we will exist in perfect harmony with our Dark Mother in flawless acausal freedom. While this is indeed a laudatory goal, it alone is insufficient.

If the fireborn and the Klifotic Elohim are successful in bringing an end to Being, as we must be, then we and God will once again have a choice. With the Ain Sof Aur and the Ain Sof Choshek reunited within the Ain Sof, the Ain Sof will finally be in a position to actualize the desire for Ain, which the suffering it has experienced will cause it to do. This will leave us with the choice to return to the Void of distinction, become the Ain Sof ourselves, or, like our God, choose Ain. A choice for anything but to follow the Path of the Serpent to Ain threatens to cause the whole cycle of suffering to continue. It is for this reason that we must set aside our A(i)nxiety and embrace the Oblivion of Impossibility. (5)

Serpent by Matthew Wightman

(5) As this article comes to a close and I prepare to submit it for publication, it occurs to me that perhaps my final conclusion may not be as inevitable as I believe. Perhaps I have uncovered a new Theology of Hope in which we are either able to return to the peace and fullness of the Void of distinction free of A(i)nxiety or to become a new Ain Sof that is free of A(i)nxiety and able to create a cosmos that is fundamentally free of the flaws of this one; a cosmos that is created only out of Love and not A(i)nxiety, that is not bound to the causal laws that this one is; one in which creation is not inclined to capitulate its inner fire to the lifeless clay of Being. Perhaps the Serpent teaches us what we need to know in order to live an existence free of the horrors that are all too common to our current reality. Then again, perhaps not. After all, if we are truly to follow the anti-cosmic path of the Serpent, should we not seek Ain for its own sake? I leave it to the reader to ponder these questions with me.

The Heirdom by Rafal kosela

The Living Atua Of The Carrefour Tarot

Sean Woodward

Night of the Zobop

"I could hear the low rumbling drone of the motor-zobop and see the swinging beams of its pale blue headlights, long before it glided slowly up the dirt track towards the crossroads. Behind me, back in the town my friends at the Institute had warned against this course of action. As a child my mother had told me stories of the night sorcerers, who drove along the midnight back roads of Port-au-Prince, abducting people for their unspeakable rites. As an older, educated man I was shaken by my inability to rid myself of the terror of her words, which seemed to grow louder in my head as the vehicle drew close, the moonlight drowning in the dull black of the hood. I resisted the urge to run and stood my ground.

"As it drew to a halt alongside me a rear door opened and a guttural voice from within beckoned. I stepped in, next to a man on the backseat, a dark fedora covering his features. The two men in the front had similar hats, similar dark suits. The interior filled with thick cigar smoke as the vehicle pulled off. The man at my side said nothing, made not a sound except for the shuffling of a deck of cards. I watched carefully as the colourful pictures moved before me in slow motion. I saw strange figures, skulls and glyphs. He stopped shuffling the cards and handed one to me. 'This will be your passport,' he said, 'keep it safe.'" —Dr. Hector Alfonse, *Memories of Saint-Domingue*, Paris 1956.

Introduction

"The Carrefour Tarot has been something that has been slowly reifying its Energy into our world for many years. Firstly, let me be clear about what the Carrefour Tarot is not. The Carrefour Tarot is not intended as a replacement or substitute for the "classic" Tarot of 78 cards. This particular deck is a Magickal Machine in and of itself. The card designs had never been published and were only described in the Monastery of the Seven Rays Year One Lessons by Michael Bertiaux. The System is a pictorial embodiment of the Syzygies and Energies of the Year One Course. Michael Bertiaux has always said that everyone should paint or create Tarots for themselves. Thinking about this I had always been surprised that no one had actually painted these designs." —Earl S. Keim III, personal correspondence, 2013.

To understand the Carrefour Tarot is to embrace the sacred space of the Crossroads and, like Dr. Alfonse, to be given a Zobop passport to the lands beyond that space. Unlike a traditional deck, this is a series of 64 cards that expresses the solar and lunar (or Archetypal) aspects of the Voudon Gnostic currents. It is not bound by a hard set of meanings and attributions and so encourages the essence of the cards to be expressed, for them to become a living map that enables travel through the Hoo, Doo and Zobop realms. It encapsulates both the concentrated energies of a Major Arcana deck and the elemental nature of the four suits of the Minor Arcana within its 16-base system of symbolism.

There are thus degrees of strength, or certainty, around the cards, for at their heart is a quantum time displacement engine which causes shifts to occur which mirror future probabilities and past influencess. This enables the deck to be used for divination. However, to limit this deck purely to the purposes of fortune telling is to limit its true potential. It has been designed as a direct result of working with the gnostic spaces that the cards represent, of opening a gateway into those realities and retrieving a symbol of their essence, to gain entry into the shifting portals to the Other-worlds. In this way the cards can be used for entering those inter-dimensional Points Chauds, for skrying and for the construction of Vudu instruments to effect reality changes.

"The Hougan Who Knows and Sees. To gain the Prize of the Eyes, the Houngan sees Invisible Existence as if he were the Great Leghba." —Michael Bertiaux, *The Monastery of the Seven Rays, IVth Year Course in Esoteric Magic*.

During the creation of the deck I began to see the importance of the Leghba and the Crossroads in the dynamics of the deck, for the four crosses rotate around the central cross of Leghba and the four cards of his astrological aspects. For this reason I named it after Carrefour, the Haitian god of magicians and lord of the crossroads, who is also called Kalfu.

History of the Carrefour Tarot

Papus, in *Tarot of the Bohemians* (1889), alludes to two ways in which the mysteries of the tarot have been preserved throughout the ages: "1. Secret societies, a direct continuation of the mysteries; 2. The cultus, a symbolic translation of the higher doctrines."

The Carrefour Tarot can be viewed in this great tradition as it is both the product of a secret society, namely Ordo Templi Orientis Antiqua and a cultus, La Couleuvre Noire. The history of the cards is linked closely with both of these vehicles of the mysteries. They are described as the Creole Cabala Tarot by Michael Bertiaux, in the initial teachings of the Monastery of the Seven Rays, and they encapsulate the energies of both of these Orders

Earl S. Keim III, in personal correspondence, says "as far as the actual System itself I advise anyone interested to consult the Monastery lessons Year One. They must be understood as Living Atua of these Energies."

The Monastery itself can be seen in the artwork of a number of the cards, such as *Archetypal Twins of the Temple*, *The Master of the Four Crosses* and *Archetypal Master of the Western Cross*. It is a pivotal location in this Creole Cabala Tarot, as it is the storehouse of the wisdom of the Orders. It is often depicted with rays emanating from one of its towers, as its energies reach out from its sanctuary space between the worlds, affecting changes in time and space, protected as it is beyond their circles. Within the Monastery amongst its many treasures are the ancient teachings of the Afro-Atlantean tradition that reaches back through time to the realm of Atlantis and Lemuria, back through space to the galaxies and star systems of Orion and Ursa Major. The stellar aspects of these traditions is mentioned by Kenneth Grant in *Cults of The Shadow* (Muller, 1972): "The Cross of the Four Quarters plus the inbetween concepts that together form the eightfold cross ... a synthetic symbol of the Goddess of the Seven Stars plus her son, Set or Sirius."

The impact of this Kosmic Vudu cartography has been felt by David Eosphorus Maples who writes in *Anomaly Report*, 2013, "I have only had the cards in my presence for one full day and already there is much to say. From the onset of the decks arrival, I could feel the otherworldly energies that emanated from its core. What I hadn't anticipated was the inward as well as outward pulls and influxes of the cosmological territory that had now been opened as a portal with these cards. I have theorised that these entities have their origin in the Sirius system. This theory is supported by the ever-present manifestation of a black dog. This dog sometimes appears in different forms, some resembled more of a jackal, and others simply a black dog adorned in gold jewellery. Since this contact, more and more cosmological entities have inhabited my space, making it their own. Watching, tempting and studying, these intelligences have a most inquiring nature, they seem to be as curious of me as I am of them. Portals and gateways into time and space have indeed been opened, and from both sides."

This Kosmic influence resonates from the trans-yuggothian spaces and is filtered by the Saturn Gnosis and the Cosmic Leghba. It is in the areas of Orion and Sirius that the source of the Afro-Atlantean and AIWAZ-Physics reside. As Michael Bertiaux states in *The Voudon Gnostic Workbook* (Weiser, 2007), "The magickal keys to the mysteries of Sirius, such as the eight unmanifest points of Sirius, ... are the power sources for the hypergeometries of the AIWAZ-physics. Contact with these entities forms an important "inner instruction" experience, in the advanced sections of AIWAZ-physics, such as "oracular topologies" and "magickal hypergeometries," etc.

"There are eight special initiations into these inner levels, which are given by means of direct contact with the entities of Sirius and in some other cases Orion (e.g., the Nemiron). The student of the inner side of magick will be admitted by means of these methods and those rays of light, which come into operation when the computer-marga is connected to the point of Sirius."

Robert Anton Wilson was another who recognised the influence of Sirius. In *Cosmic Trigger* (Falcon Press, 1986), he states, "On 23 July 1973, I had the impression that I was being contacted by some sort of advanced intellect from the system of the double star Sirius. I have had odd psychic experiences of that sort for many years, and I always record them carefully, but refuse to take any of them literally, until or unless supporting evidence of an objective nature turns up. This particular experience, however, was especially staggering, both intellectually and emotionally, so I spent the rest of the day at the nearest large library researching Sirius. I found, among other things, that 23 July is very closely associated with that star."

Kenneth Grant identifies the planet Emme Ya in the star system of Sirius as the home of the Loa in *Hecate's Fountain* (Skoob, 1992). Orion is the herald of Sirius-LAM. The influence of LAM to La Coulelvere Noire (LCN) has been explained by Michael Bertiaux in Kenneth Grant's *Cults of the Shadow:* "LAM, without a doubt this is the same being who worked with Lucien Francois, Jean-Maine when the latter organised the work of the LCN in the 1920s."

The Monastery is regularly visited by Masters and Hierophants, by novices and mages who have found the mountainous path to its door. The Abbé Boullan returned to it from journeys to Orion. The Monastery can be likened to the home of the Secret Chiefs in Karl von Eckartshausen's *The Cloud Upon The Sanctuary* (1895), or the Perilous Chapel of Arthurian Myth. This, however, is also a very Haitian system, including as it does motifs of the Vodou spirits or Loa of Port-au-Prince, Jacmel and Leogane. These are reflected in cards depicting the Twins or Marassa, Leghba and the Guedhe family of Loa.

This tarot originated in the development of the esoteric faculty of La Prise des Yeaux during an intense period of exploration of the realms of the Hoo Spirits. These were opened following contact with the Loa, which enabled the artistic form of the cards to take shape. The Loa also enabled an environment conducive to the reception and production of the cards to arise, without which they could not have been published. In many ways they are a very personal vision; however, it is a vision shaped by the communications and explorations of these Hoo realms or Gnostic Spaces. It is from this direct interaction with such spaces that the dynamic power and resonation of the tarot comes. It is born from experience, from working day in and day out with the forces, of learning how to communicate their essence in a form which will itself unfold its nature to those who work closely with it.

The Initiate of the Northern Cross by Sean Woodward

When working with the HooDoo realms in this manner, the Loa or Les Mystères themselves often guided me. Milo Rigaud in *Secrets of Voodoo* (New York, 1969) expresses this: "The Mystères themselves give the instruction by "mounting" someone, who then instructs the initiate verbally. Otherwise the Mystères send him dreams or visions when necessity arises. A great many Houn'gans are created in this supernatural manner. It is the Loas themselves who initiate them and give them the Asson."

It is clear that the Loa are able to use the medium of art in this way as a direct line of communication. As Kyle Fite states in *Vessels of Vision - The Gnostic Artist as Magician of the Crossroads* (OTOA Public Papers Series, 2013), "Every member of this Cultus, whether he knows himself as such or not, is busy fashioning windows and gates into the Otherworld. Like Jacob's ladder, powers from Beyond pass to and fro via these turnstyles. Matter is becoming Spirit and Spirit is becoming Matter. These sublime transformations are not unlike William Blake's view towards "a world in a grain of sand" and "Heaven in a wild flower." Passing through these Gates is not an arduous task. It is simply a shifting of inner vision. As the New World comes into focus, we discover a proliferation of possibilities and a Vessel of Endless Vision to those who would partake of the same."

These are a system of worlds brought forth via a Voudon Cabala of the Higher Consciousness, of entering into the Vudu continuum, of travelling to the inner retreat of the masters of light and entering into an arcane zombie trance state that allowed its colours to permeate my very being. It is a picture book brought back from ancient-time and future-time, a high class occult decadence!

Others who have experienced the vibrancy of the Voudon Gnostic current also attest to the close relationship between art and magick. David Beth states in *Voudon Gnosis* (Fulgur, 2010), "producing art as part of ritual became strongly connected to this cult as the initiates drew more and more powers and pictures from the world of the spirits... he is able to develop a coherent map of the magical universe, inner and outer, and allow a progressive mystical and magical development. It is not unusual to see the temple of a Voudon Gnostic initiate filled with art and creative objects which are representations and reconstructions of his inner plane experiences."

Unlike the static imagery and meanings of the traditional tarot, the Carrefour Tarot is not based on the fixed repetition of Hermetic attributions, themselves pinned to the Kabbalistic world-view of the Tree of Life, but pulled from the torrential living river and waters of Ville Au Champs, the underwater home world of the Loa.

It is a quantum tarot, an encoding of the changing forces that underpin the form of the worlds.

This is a tarot of the Four Crosses. These are the four great watchtowers known to Dr. Dee that delineate the boundaries of the universe. At their heart is the creation and destruction of form, the interaction of the Initiates and Hierophants as time and space and chance are bent in and out of shape. In this inter-dimensional cosmic flux, walk the Loa, the Marassa and other Nations, robed in the catastrophic birth and death of millennia. These are the ancestors who have embraced their ancient Atlantean birthrights, who guide us in the uncovering of their treasures and the revelation of our own natures. They work throughout the centuries in union with the Gros Bon Ange and Ti Bon Ange of every devotee of the Cult of the Black Snake (La Coulevere Noire), ensuring that the Great Work of the illumination of mankind never falters and the dawning of a day when once more mankind walks amidst the stars becomes less distant.

It is this aeonic flux that is so poorly described in the structure of all other tarots. Look at the static design of so many and you will see its omission. It is as if the characters posed in a photographer's studio. Only a few, such as 'The Magician' or 'The World', show any attempt at movement, of embracing the dance of of life.

Wether it is the artistic, geometric beauty of Crowley's Thoth or the picture book gentleness of the Rider-Waite, they are each wrapped in a linear ribbon of activity. Symbolically they are nailed to the paths and sephirah of the Dayside Tree and know nothing of the true duality that holds the pylons of Mercy and Severity in place. Only in the invisible energies of Daath is there an inkling of the true foundation of this system, of the gateway that passes between all the worlds. It is here, in the dark sephirah of the Carrefour that the building blocks of the universe whirl about the four great crosses.

Carrefour Syzygies by Sean Woodward

Emblems and Motifs of the Crossroads

As a tarot derived from Vudu Gnostic teachings, this deck contains a number of dynamic Vudu motifs. There are four forms of Leghba, the guardian of the Crossroads. The Twins are the Marassa and in the Initiate cards we see something of the Guedhe family of Loa. The Black Snake of the cultus appears in two of the cards.

It is this Vudu nature of the cards that is one of its greatest strengths as these are some of the oldest forms and guardians of the tradition. It is true that it is both Vodoun and Gnostic, but there is a raw energy in the Voudon elements, whose frantic dance can sometimes dislodge the finery of Gnostic robes. The Loa demand the full attention of their devotees, and whilst they may proffer differing levels of possession, it is certain that they will manifest this. In its most delicate form, the adept retains their consciousness but it is clear that it has been altered momentarily by the presence of another. This can be of the subtlest nature, a sudden change in one's preferences and temperament, a sudden yearning for objects of attention previously without consideration, or a return to a more primal state. This is the type of consciousness we cultivate for divination as it does not involve the complete subjugation of mind and body but enables the adept to remain conscious and to retain dominion, whilst transmitting the knowledge of the Loa.

Many of the cards, such as 'The Server of the Eastern Cross' or 'The Master of the Western Cross', are representations of the Crossroads Cross itself, each with a different aspect depending upon its quarter of manifestation. Of course, in each of the Leghba cards there is a huge cross in the background. The cross in its simplest form is made of these two arms of alternate forces, the male and female, the Ying and Yang, the Marassa themselves.

Another important symbol in this deck is the cross which is surrounded by smaller crosses and circles. I was first exposed to the energies of this Palo Mayombe symbol in Havana. Though primarily a symbol of Zarabanda, it is also a glyph of the universe and speaks to me of the Crossroads and the gateway it provides between the worlds. The cross and circle appears in the chokers and armbands in these depictions of the Loa. It represents their status and mastery of the dual forces which shape the nature of all existence.

Nicholaj De Mattos Frisvold, in personal correspondence, explains the use of this symbology in the construction of firmas or patiepembas, the Palo Moyambe equivalents of veves, "the +o patterns are used to present a cosmic and creative condition ranging from being and potency for becoming—hence being a vital building block for making a firma come alive and transmit meaning, this technology and how these patterns are used, constructed and recognized, is not supposed to be discussed outside the nzo."

A key identifier of the Archetypal cards is the spiral motif of the Zobop. Whilst these are the lunar aspects of the cards, they contain a dynamic energy from the Nightside Tree or Universe-B.

Finally, the design on the back of the cards incorporates a number of personal and universal Vudu glyphs. XVI is for the 16 degrees and Points Chauds. There is a skull for Guedhe. The S and Z characters are a personal glyph and exoterically represent the cosmic trans-yuggothic energies of Sirius-Sothis and Zothyrius.

The Ritual of Opening the Crossroads

The Crossroads is not confined to a dusty intersection on the outskirts of town, where once passing old bluesmen might impart a little of the wisdom borne of a life of wandering and earthly experience. It is a sacred space that can be formed in the corner of a room, by the earth beneath our feet, at a table or altar or in any place the adept desires because the influence of the Spirits is not limited to the areas of migration of the Afro-Atlantean tradition, but rather to the subtle environs of the adept.

This is best explained by the Sovereign Grand Master of the OTOA-LCN (Coils I.III, 2013): "Michael Bertiaux once shared with me that the Haitian Spirits attached to the Jean-Maine Familie took an interest in America and thus 'migrated' here. This was done via Bertiaux himself who had been selected as a Vehicle of the Spirits. These Spirits 'inhabited' our Orders as a functional 'Body'."

To achieve the latter, simply cross the fingers of both hands, as if making the common gesture for wishing good luck, and then bring the hands together to form another cross of the four fingers. In doing so you are invoking the power of the four great crosses of the Carrefour Tarot. Part the hands, make a petition to Leghba to open the Crossroads between the worlds in this very spot and then uncross your fingers. The opening is complete. This same process can be followed in reverse to close the space. It should be noted, however, that unlike the acts of ceremonial magic, the Lucky Hoodoo is not obsessed with the banishing of the spirits. Rather, they are invited into the initiate's life, where their strength and support can be felt. In Haitian

Vodou one "walks with the Loa." This is a relationship built upon mutual respect and friendship.

Magick of the Carrefour Tarot

The four great crosses of the Carrefour tarot represent directions in both time and space. Lay down the signifier card—this is usually 'The Magician of the Red Triangle' or 'The Magician of the Blue Triangle' depending on your gender. Then, lay out the four Leghba cards in a cross around these and recite the Petition of the Crossroads. Finally, lay out the necessary cards to effect the change you desire.

The Six Secret Signifiers.

The first edition of the tarot also includes six Signifier cards that were originally designed for use by members of Ordo Templi Orientis Antiqua and La Couluvere Noire. These act as replacement signifiers to the standard ones, each a totem of special energies. They are titled 'FA Hat of the Houngan', 'Gran Bois', 'Carrefour', 'Gros Bon Ange', 'Bacalou Baca' and 'Spider Loa'. They can be used to replace the Signifier card in divination and as focal points for meditation, skrying or Vudu time travel. The Spider Loa card is particularly suited to the latter as it can represent the spider sorcerer form employed by the initiate in Le Temple Des Houdeaux. Further details of the Temple can be found in *The Voudon Gnostic Workbook* by Michael Bertiaux (Weiser, 2007).

Vudu Hermetics and Divination

"There are sixty-four Ontic spheres which are universal conditions. Each Ontic sphere is composed of four spaces, which explicate the gnostic energies of the Ontic sphere. The rulers of the Ontic spheres have magical and gnostic authority over the rulers of the spaces of light." —Michael Bertiaux, *The Magical Geography of Master Michael Aquarius* (Sanctuary Teachings, 1981) The 16-fold system that underpins this tarot is related to the IFA number sequences of 4, 8, 16, 32, 64, etc. These numbers grow and shrink into each other, and it is this momentum that drives the quantum engine at the core of this tarot.

Whilst the Voudon Gnostic current is very different from those experienced in the western traditions, the 16-fold energies do have echoes in the hermetic models.

"The Magician of the Sixteen FA is the master of human history, for all of mankind's efforts pass under sixteen magical symbols of the FA." —Michael Bertiaux, *Monastery of the Seven Rays Year 1*.

The 32 cards can be mapped to the 32 degrees of Masonry and to the 32 divisions of the Tree of Life. The Manifest cards relate to the Dayside tree, the Archetypal ones to the Nightside tree. In a similar fashion pairs of I-Ching hexagrams can be assigned, e.g., Hexagrams 1 and 2 to the 1st Sephirah, 63 and 64 to the 32nd path, enabling these to be mapped to the Kabbalistic model. To determine the manner of this map, the order of the tarot as described in the Monastery papers should be employed, e.g.:

The 16 cards governed by Racine - a. The Master of the northern cross. b. The twins of the Temple. c. The Master of the Four Crosses. d. Legba Capricorn. e. Legba Scorpio f. The Master of the western cross. g. The twins of the ritual design. h. The magician of the blue triangle. i. The twins of the centre post. j. Legba Aquarius. k. The Master of the southern cross. 1. The magician of the sixteen FA. m. The twins of the altar. n. The magician of the red triangle. o. Legba Leo p. The Master of the eastern cross.

The 16 cards governed by Padern - a. The initiate of the northern cross. b. The server of the northern cross. c. The priest of the northern cross. d. The hierophant of the northern cross. e. The initiate of the western cross. f. The server of the western cross. g. The priest of the western cross. h. The hierophant of the western cross. i. The initiate of the southern cross. The server of the southern cross. k. The priest of the southern cross. 1. The hierophant of the southern cross. m. The initiate of the eastern cross. n. The server of the eastern cross. c. The priest of the eastern cross. p. The hierophant of the eastern cross.

The main cards are in a state of Manifest Active Expression whilst the others are in Archetypal or Abstract form. This division enables a determination to be made in divination as to how the subject relates to these energies and powers and to the nature of situations. As the majority of the cards are assigned to the four great crosses, the elemental attributes of the directions can be explored for divinatory meaning. For simpler divination, the Manifest cards generally represent "Yes," the Archetypal ones "No."

The Twins of the Ritual Design by Sean Woodward

Dean Crowder, in personal correspondence, gives an example of practical use of the deck. "What I do is ask a question and then I am usually directed to count a specific number of cards down. This is not something I normally do, but it has been occurring a lot since I started using this deck. I always draw cards one at a time and usually only work with a few per question (I don't use spreads). Whichever card comes up is naturally met with resistance because I have no idea what the card 'means'. So, instead of worrying about this I use the artwork itself to see symbols and images, sort of like scrying. A curve here, a twist there is enough to inspire the intuitional leaps that shake out the answer."

Carrefour Cartographies

It is the leapers of the Nightside of the Tree who deliver the codices and cartographies of the gnosis. In the Hoo form of the frog or toad they are able to jump the vast dark spaces between the power zones, as snakes and fish swim the flooded tunnels that burrow through the worlds. Echoes of their words are heard by the sorcerers of the English Vudu, glimpses of their body tattoos manifesting in backwards written glyphs and sigils. These can be seen in both forms of the 'Leghba Scorpio' card where they appear in the deep spaces behind the cross of Leghba. In the 'Master of the Four Crosses' card, the four great crosses themselves have become sigil forms and erupt from his very speech. In the 'Archetypal Master of the Western Cross' card, they have become an emblem, part of his badge of office. In every case, from 'The Twins of the Centre Post' to the 'Archetypal Server of the Northern Cross' cards, it is these sigils which add to the talismanic nature of the deck and both power and become manifestations of the quantum displacement engine which is at the heart of the deck. The cards are a map of the Voudon territories and letters of introduction to the intelligences that inhabit them.

"It was many years before I was able to hold in my own hands the cards that I had seen that dark night, to feel not just the Zobop energies which coursed through them, but the shinning pulsar, the living Atua of the gnosis of Leghba. Through all that time I kept in my waistcoat pocket that card I had been given, for it was a great signifier of the mysteries that would open to me." —Dr. Hector Alfonse, *Memories of Saint-Domingue*, Paris 1956.

Sean Woodward *is an initiate of OTOA-LCN and has created the Carrefour Tarot in service to the Monastery of the Seven Rays and the establishment of the Evolving Empire of the Hoodoo Spirits. He was a member of the Nephthys Arachna Power Zone and is the Knight Diplomatis Supreme of Society OTO. His art and writing have been published internationally, appearing in Lamp of Thoth, Zhoupheus and Estronomicon. He is represented by ZOSHOUSE | FINE-ART and his tarot and art may be viewed at* www.seanwoodward.com

Master of the Words of the Island Under The Sea by Sean Woodward

Sigil Inversion and Qliphothic Gestalt

Robert Podgurski

Austin Spare was emphatic regarding the reification of desires through his prescribed technique of sigils. The sigil once formulated for manifesting that desire is then projected deep into the subconscious void. Typically an expressed desire, no matter its sublime nature, is still a product of jagrat, the tonal waking state. Furthermore, it is enticing to consider what may be attained through summoning sigils from those very depths to inform and guide us in gaining some understanding of the pool of unadulterated desire.

Gaining awareness of such sigil mechanisms is a process that may take on a variety of approaches depending on one's perspective. Like water itself the subconscious maintains a delicate surface tension, a membrane that sustains the dividing line between above and below, everyday awareness and shadow consciousness. This membrane is there for the creative play of the magician, and the permeability, presence, absence, and detection thereof is what lies at the core in such a magical operation.

Qliphoth Opus III

It is easy to relegate the shadow or qliphothic realm to a mysterious and somewhat elusive patch of consciousness; however, it is readily accessible to the open eye that may conceive the gestalt of this interplay between the void and the physical sphere.

Order vs. _____

The notion of any type of interpretation of qliphothic activity is contra naturam. Explication of shadow world consciousness is an attempt to bring the dark-side of the cosmos into the light of consciousness. However the means whereby the practitioner is bound to communicate this experience is by its very nature bound to fall short of the mark. Approximations, always approximations delimited by the analogue.

What should be of paramount concern to the qliphothic magician is the essence of the transmission which is not always geared to a verbal interpretation, hence the subheading of this section. Leaving a blank as opposed to supplying the obvious, Order vs. Chaos or Order vs. Formlessness is indicative of what I am driving at, the loaded pregnant blank to be filled in by the imagination is far more vast in its implications than one word or signifier is capable of alluding to.

It may be argued that such a title is imprecise, vague, even distracting. However, given the difficult task of conceptualizing the qliphoth I would argue that it is open-ended in an attempt to represent the very amorphous and vacuous condition that is associated with immersion in these dark recesses of consciousness.

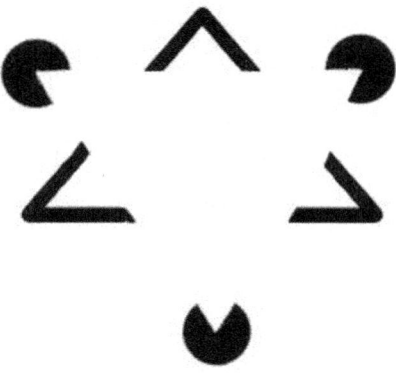

Closure 2 by Robert Podgurski

In fact, the non-assertion of "Order vs. ____" demonstrates the antithesis of the gestalt law of closure.

Typically this law refers to visual images such as squares or circles depicted by broken lines thereby asserting that even though parts are missing the components that are present still represent the whole as perception assembles it from the sensory data on-hand. Instead, the open phrase represents the antithesis of this law and ventures into not only demonstrating but activating an awareness of a quantum entangled system. In the field of Quantum Cognition, where quantum mechanics theories are seen as concomitant with gestalt perceptual processes, a quantum entangled system is said to be explicative of a word's associative network such as occurs in free-association exercises made popular during the sixties, etc.

For the qliphothic magician this realm networks from the conscious realm of associations through the subconscious or pre-conscious phases of awareness. The gestalt fuzz-trace theory posits that information is encoded in either verbatim traces or gist traces, the latter being the more significant in the qliphothic context.

Gist traces are conceptual, free-associative, connotative, allusive components that the mind latches onto through flights of fancy, aesthetics, etc. Subsequently, that is why I chose to leave the opposing factor to "Order" unspecified so that the reader is free to fill in that blank. It is that filling-in process that touches upon the crux of moving from a purely analytic mode of gestalt perceptual theorizing toward an active means of access and kriya (action) for the qliphothic magician. I am suggesting here a series of techniques for gaining access to a level of awareness where shadow-consciousness may emerge to provide the essential tools for revealing itself.

For the most part in the western tradition, access to qliphothic gateways and extra dimensions has been facilitated through the use of sigils, chants, etc.

For instance, the qliphothic genii of the 22 cells of the reverse side of the tree of life were brought to the fore in Crowley's Liber 231. In this system there is an acknowledged referent to a Cabalistic sphere of influence and its shadow or dark side. There is in essence a verbatim, i.e., Tarotic attribution, as well as a gist trace of reference from which the magician may look upon as a recognizable starting point.

The destination, however, reveals itself through the meditative process. The principle quandary for the aspirant then is which qliphothic cell to work with. And once the initial decision to undertake exploration of the shadow paths has been committed to then it is more often than not advantageous to exercise intuition as to where one may gain the most advantageous foothold to commence with. Furthermore, as with certain paths, such as the Voudonic, the option of facilitating the subconscious, i.e., qliphothic space, to assist in making the choice is optimal.

The loa of the Voudonic pantheon are said to ride, or possess, the practitioner, but before the ride may commence consciousness must be groomed and conditioned to accept the mount and eventual direction set by the dark spirit. By reversing much of the processes of traditional western magick this receptive and focused condition may be acquired simply and systematically.

Typically, the implementation of sigils in the modern sense follows an apparent procedure. First the desire or objective is articulated, then it is transferred to a sigil, graphic and or aural, that bears little or no resemblance to the expressed desire. In adhering to Austin Spare's system, sigils are constructed in this manner so that they may pass more seemlessly into the subconscious so as to avoid unwanted interference posed by the machinations of the conscious mind. However, in order to access and explore qliphothic forces, following the process in a somewhat reversed process may prove very beneficial to the practitioner so inclined.

Re-emergence from the Depths

In Lvx tenebrae. In the light of darkness for the qliphothic magician; moreover, what better place to acquire the sigils themselves but from this reservoir of the infinite. To enable this process, I have developed an exercise that provides an expedient method. First of all, this technique permits ample room for modification and revision to suit the practitioner's specific needs or proclivities. Initially, I visualize an entrance to a cave with a large gate to it on my physical backside. Since the qlipa have been conceptualized as the tunnels of set, I find a cave conducive as an access point. Those who have a greater affinity to water, for example, may choose to visualize a dark bottomless pool, etc.

Once I see the cave entrance, I knock upon the gate and declare my request: "I desire a sigil for entry to a qliphoth that I should work with." Notice, the emphasis is on "should" and this is key because it leaves all conscious desires and infatuations at the door, so to speak. I wait to see if the gate opens. If it doesn't, I choose another meditation.

I find it is best not to force entry; the Goddess doesn't appreciate it. When the gate parts, I put out my hand and wait to be guided forth into the depths. Sometimes I see a figure, sometimes I merely sense a guiding force from the shadows. Then, as I am led into the tunnels I pay close attention to the details of the area on my descent. This attention to minutiae is excellent work for the magical memory, etc.

Once I have been led to wherever it is I am supposed to be, and usually I find it is another chamber or gate that must be opened, then I enter and see what sigil is revealed to me. I then typically ask how should I use the sigil and why. The critical question is "why." I have learned an immense amount from this approach and what is most critical here is that this practice is such a valuable time-saver. Before developing this method, I would find myself occasionally working with energies that proved ineffective or draining because I was not attuned to what the shadow world was beckoning me to access. This approach has fostered a new degree of receptivity and ease of path working that I had not known before, not to mention eliminating a lot of guessing as well as trial and error.

The beauty of this technique is that it works well with just about any approach to qliphotic magick, be it Crowleyan-based tunnels of set, Necronomicon-related magick, Voudon, etc. For a little more in-depth analysis I will site some examples of my own findings. I myself work with a myriad of systems; however, since I first started with the 22 qliphothic cells of the tree of life as established by Crowley in his Liber 231 and developed an affinity for it early on, I typically return to it time and time again as a base point of reference.

And so I will often enter into the cave inquiring as to which of these qliphothic tunnels I should work with. For example, I recently embarked on one of these exercises and found myself directed to a space where I had a cat's cradle-like weave of energy between my hands, detecting currents of fusion and blending in silence, no verbal type messages. I then surmised that I was in the tunnel Gargophias. As is evident, the sigil for Gargophias is one of the most symmetrical ones depicted by Crowley in Liber 231.

This symmetry, combined with the antithesis of the oracular priestess, all paralleled and reinforced my received directive. The next day, during a dawn meditation I saw myself drawing an infinity symbol over a picture. Again, another symmetrical graphic indicating the current initiated. Without going into great detail about my own personal revelations through meditation on these received images, I will say that the most germane result of this working was an expanded perspective and awareness of this tunnel that I had never touched on before. This symmetry—it became clear, or awareness thereof connected with the simple fact that Gargophias/The Priestess splits the middle of the tree facilitating symmetry.

Gargophias by Robert Podgurski

    This dividinline, or tunnel as it were, is where the two sides meet at a seamless point. That imperceptible line is the space that defies verbal articulation, hence the root and or antithesis of the oracular—the unique expanded perception that only muted speech imparts.
    Even though sigils act upon the subconscious strata differently than symbols or words do upon the conscious mind, there does appear to be a type of shadow syntax that underscores their functioning. This is not to say that the ordering of the parts, the lines, curves, etc., form a syntactical ordering as words do in sentences.
    Since sigils act in a latent capacity then their shape, design, order of execution are indicative of traces of how the subconscious functions as a dark organism, respiring, feeding, growing, encompassing and fusing with others of its kind and acting as a shadow mirror of the known universe. If at this point I must rely upon less than exact analogies, it is not surprising given the topic at hand. Language can be a poor servant in matters of the sublime and that which is naught. Or as Robert Duncan so well described, "As if I could cast a shadow that surrounds what is boundless."
    Words operate as shadows of meaning and, in this case, meanings that are representative of shadows of things to be described in language:

obscurum per ad obscurum. Nonetheless, there are certain insights to be gained given these rudimentary implements.

The syntactical arrangement of words in sentences in language is such that it effects a common patterning that is universally identifiable amongst speakers of that language so that structure facilitates the imparted meaning. The components of sigils operate similarly but not in precisely the same manner.

The audience of a given sigil is more narrow. In short, the sigil is a sign that permits the communication and reification of desire between the conscious and subconscious minds. As a result the rules of syntax are far less rigid or defined but rather exceedingly intrinsic and even idiosyncratic when it comes to each and every person's implementation of sigils. Because of this narrow relationship, we are by necessity bound to dealing with allusions and connotations as opposed to explicative hard and fast set parameters, such as is evidenced in verbal systems of communication.

Traditionally, Yantras are constructed from the bindu, or seed, at the center first then proceeding to the outermost perimeter. The meditation on the Yantra then follows the reverse order from outside to inside, i.e., innermost awareness. In this qliphothic sigil formation technique I described in the previous section, the practitioner takes this process to the next level by accessing and evoking the sigil from the inner temenos.

Now in analyzing, or rather, intuiting the actual components of the sigil through any extant system, the aspirant is more apt to benefit from devising their own catalog of shapes, configurations, etc., of basic elements of sigil design and what these elements signify. For instance, in *Destiny and Control in Human Systems*, Charles Muses established a chart of human phosphenes and what they connote.

Austin Spare himself actually developed a small chart of similar attributes.

However, like dream interpretation my sense is that the significance of any design and its corresponding allusions must be performed on an individual basis, and that any attempt to standardize such qualifications is bound to be problematic

These factors must be felt and psychometrized for one to adumbrate an accurate breakdown of these designs for one's personal magical use.

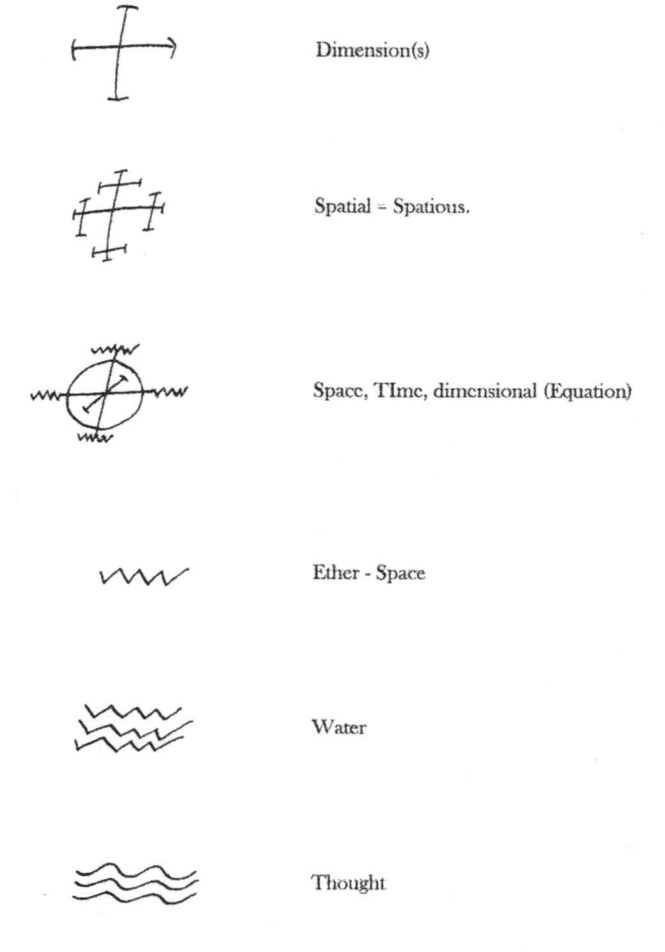

Fig. 11. Austin Osman Spare's sigils for time and space from: Grant, Kenneth and Steffi. <u>Zos Speaks: Encounters with Austin Osman Spare</u>. Oxford, England: Fulgur Limited, 1998. p. 124 .

Spares gridlike sigils

Rank Number	Occurrence Frequency (%)	Phosphene Form-Types (with variants)	Semantic Connotations
1	21.5		interfacing of two and more systems into a larger whole
2	16.6		ray radiation
3	15.4		wave-organization
4	13.0		basic structure and central support
5	9.6		wave-radiation from a center
6	8.8		ulitimate seeds or particles
7	>3.5		completed, reciprocal balance
8	3.5		power release
9	<3.5		pairing, reflection, fissioning
10	1.8		controllability and positioning (by coordinates)
11	1.5		released or freed unit or quantum form (triangle is minimal-edge enclosure)
12	1.3		rhythm and development by successive reaction (wave generation

The Set of Human Phosphenes in Order of Decreasing Frequency

Fig. 19. Charles Muses Phosphene table 4-3 from <u>Destiny and Control in Human Systems</u> pp. 110-111..

Muses chart

Nonetheless, I find Dee's Monas Hieroglyphica a good starting point from which to chart basic elements. The first two theorems of the Monas Dee stated that the ray, line, and circle all evolved from the point. Regardless of which system one may be working from, I've found Dee's first two theorems to hold relatively constant and universal.

The bindu is also referred to as the "first circuit" or "nadi." It is actually the decentered center that may be found everywhere. Its expansion gives rise to the ray or line—continuum or nada. That line can then expand or be altered to offer magnitude and dimension—parmineya, taking on a negative or positive polarity, i.e., centrifugal or centripetal force. The Bindu in its expansion gives rise to the eight directions of space (Khana 98, 102). Also, the Bindu finds its parallel within the Cabalistic doctrine of the Zim Zum. The Zim Zum doctrine, briefly, is similar to the big bang theory in that it represents the contraction of the primal void and its infinite expansion as giving rise to the universe (The Sacred Alignments and Dark Side of Sigils, 53).

I have cited this section from my book, *The Sacred Alignments,* to provide a general overview of how I view the ontology of these basic elements, line, circle, point and their relation to certain universals. When these curves, lines, etc., are combined to establish the sigil, one may derive the added benefit of what certain combined attributions may suggest about the nature of the sigil and the desire the magician is looking to materialize.

I am being careful not to state that this approach will "define" because we are dealing with sigils and not language. Yet these are universally recognized components of form—lines, points, rays, etc.—that in essence help bridge the gap between sigil and symbol. Sigils are themselves a communication tool but one that is a medium between the conscious and macrocosmic being: the one that makes things happen. Obviously, the way things happen or become manifest is not always by way of a set ordered format, hence the fluid and open nature of sigils.

These very dynamics are what in turn allows for the search for this syntax to move beyond sigils themselves to the surrounding life-patterning of the magician. Since the subconscious is the repository of all that we know and do, it is reasonable to assume that an understanding of the syntax of our literal movement may be connected to the sigils each of us devises for our own usage. From the point one begins to grapple with ones desire to the stage where that desire is given a sigilic representation, there is motion, breathing, walking, etc.

One worthwhile meditation in this respect is to replay in the mind's screen one's physical movement that occurred between feeling the desire and creating the sigil. The actual physical pattern as seen from above, where we walked, did, moved our arms, legs, etc., as a great speculum of the mindful body at play in action. How one talked, physical sense of being, energy levels, and actual pattern that one followed while walking that day can tell us how we arrived at the sigil and what was leading us to it.

Being moved by the spirit in this sense is not just a figurative allusion but a substantive and active one. This pattern is itself a magical map/sigil matrix that may be used for a variety of exploratory methods only limited by the magician's imagination or inhibitions. As the tantric method of constructing yantras typically follows the movement of starting at the center and working outwards to the perimeter.

Then the meditative process takes the reverse path of focusing on the perimeter of the yantra and then gradually bringing the attention to its center or figurative inner-most realms of awareness. Based on this mode of logic, the meditation I am suggesting looks at one's life movement as forming a yantra worthy of being implemented as a tool for raising consciousness. The contiguity between basic mundane activities and the spiritual path is a key, and commonly overlooked nexus that is pregnant with significance to the qliphothic magician.

A practical application of this theory is to sit with pen in hand and begin tracing the aforementioned path taken without looking at the design being created as is done with automatic drawing. I choose to meditate on the path, my movements, etc., while executing the drawing. This drawing is in a sense a sacred map theoretically similar to Austin Spare's sacred alphabet. It is not a literal map but an automatic cartographical exposé of the body and soul's motion en route to sigil formation/discovery. We as chaos and qliphothic magicians do not operate in an isolated bubble.

The activity preceding the formation of a sigil, ritual, etc., is all part and parcel of the magical act which is timeless. Truly powerful magical acts have their origins a priori as well as a posteriori, or in the words of the archangel Gabriel: "Magick worketh effects in things absent, that it doeth in their parts, being present" (T&FR 117). Deja Vu is often an indicator of the atemporal nature of the magical act.

Once the magical map/yantra has been constructed it then can be used as a sigil or as a traditional type of yantra for further meditation. In certain ways this automap(ic) drawing is a unique hybrid tool. It is different from traditional yantras and sigils but these analogues are the closest points of reference and so I have referred to them for ease of understanding. Nonetheless, I believe it is far more useful to let the tool dictate its use to the magician. Therefore, once one has constructed an automap then I would suggest meditating upon it and letting it convey exactly how it is to be implemented by the magician, and asking what it is for, treating it as a living entity and it will respond.

Robert Podgurski

Works Cited

Duncan, Robert. Bending the Bow. New York: New Directions, 1968.

Dee, John. A True and Faithful Relation. Ed. Meric Casaubon D. D., 1659. North Wales, England:

The Golden Dragon Press, 1974.

Monas Heiroglyphica. Reproduced in "A Translation of John Dee's Monas

Heiroglyphica" (Antwerp 1564)." Ed. C. H. Josten. Ambix 12 (1964): 84-221.

Muses, Charles. Destiny and Control in Human Systems.

Boston: Kluwer Academic Publishers, 1985.

Podgurski, Robert The Sacred Alignments and Dark Side of Sigils.

Louth, England: Mandrake Press, Ltd., 2012.

Spare, Austin Osman. Zos Speaks: Encounters With Austin Osman Spare.

England: Fulgur Press Limited, 1988.

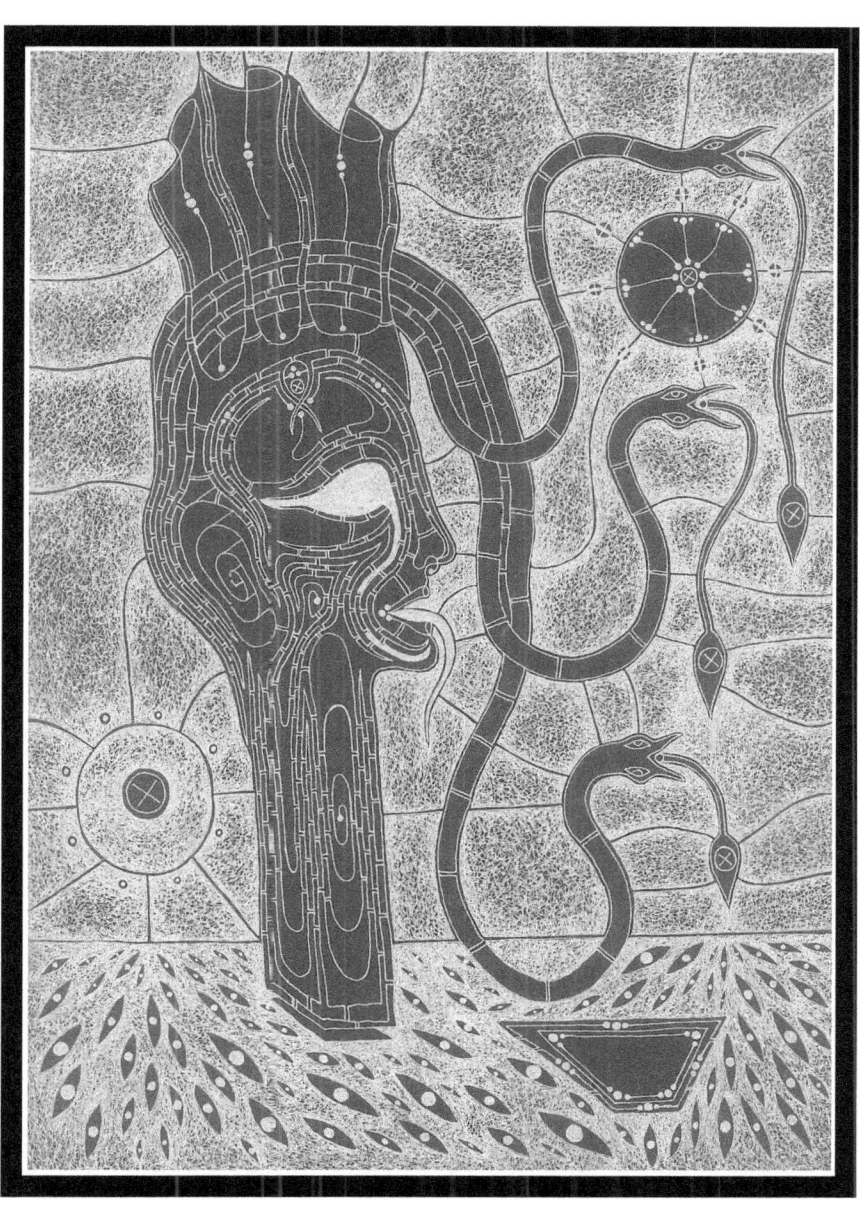

A.Y.V.V.V.A.S by rafal kosela

Kali: The Womb Of Death And Void

Daemon Barzai

Kali is a complex Goddess with lots of qualities. She is a lovely mother but also cruel and bloodthirsty. On the Cabalistic Tree of the Night she is related to Gamaliel, the Dark side of the Moon, but we can also find her on Satariel, the Saturnine Qlipha. It doesn't stop here, can't because she is also the Womb of the Universe, the Void beyond Thaumiel, there where the Womb of the Dragon is.

A meeting with Kali could be a rewarding yet very traumatic experience. As initiatrix, she is a marvelous teacher; she can teach and initiate us into the mysteries only known by those who have lived the experience.

The ritual below, it's a trip to one's death, a transformation rite, a rebirth into the Womb of the Goddess. This experience could be traumatic and painful, but at the same time, rewarding. Here, Kali will be our guide into the Void.

The Ritual

Decorate your personal altar with things that remind you of the link with death, e.g., black and red candles, skulls, bones, a Kali statue and her Yantra.

Sometimes, Kali may ask for blood, in which case you can use your own blood for this ritual, but this is not mandatory. Another useful element for this ritual is a "Japa Mala". Good incenses like roses or sandalwood will help you to tune your mind in with the Goddess.

When you are ready, light the candles and the incenses, drop some of your blood on Kali's Yantra and repeat 108 times Kali's mantra, focusing your attention on the Kali's Yantra. Once you are finished doing this, begin with the invocation.

The Invocation

AUM KRING KALIKAYE NAMAH AUM (X 108)

Melez!

May the ritual begin!

Kali, Kali Ma, Kali Ka!

Come to me powerful Goddess!

Mistress of Life and Death!

Let me know the mysteries that guard your Black Womb!

Kali: The Womb Of Death And Void

Lead me beyond Death and Life!

Let me know the glory that hides you Primal Void!

Tear down the veil of illusions and let me experience the joy of your entire being!

On the Void lies your truly power and face!

A face that only could be seen by the chosen ones!

Endow me with your power and let me do this trip guided by your wisdom!

As well you perform a Cosmic Dance over your consort Shiva

I ask you that you perform your Cosmic Dance over me!

Defeating any witness on me!

I want to emerge rebirth from your Black Womb

On the Void Heart

On the Power of the Dragon!

Kali (magical name) I call you through the names:

Durga

Badrakali

Sati

Rudrani

Parvati

Chinnamasta

Chamunda

Kamakshi

Uma

Meenakshi

Himavati

Kumari

Tara

Kali

In the name of the Dragon!

So mo it be!

The Meditation

After the invocation, meditate for a while on the meaning of Kali and her energy. When you feel ready, begin with the meditation. Relax your body, close your eyes and start to visualize a cemetery. The place is old, it's late at night and a bright full moon is illuminating the place. Walk for a while, and you see a smoke from a crematory coming from afar: go there. On the crematory's doors there is the Kali's Yantra; put your hand on it and say the words *"Lepaca Kliffoth"*. The door opens and your go in. Lie down on the ashes and begin to whisper the name Kali. After a while, she appears in front of you, her face and body covered in blood. She has a necklace with heads, and in each hand she holds a pitchfork, a sword, a spear and a skull with blood. She drinks from the skull and gives it to you, drink from it. The experience is ecstatic, powerful and overwhelming. She asks if you are ready for the trip; when you feel ready, say yes. She begins to cut your body; this is a painful process. When she finishes, your spirit releases and you can see the flesh of your body lying there, but it's dead. A Black Vortex opens in front of you and you are swallowed by it. Inside the Vortex you can't see anything, just blackness. After a moment, Kali appears in front of you and she guides you on this trip. Enjoy the experience and keep your mind open to the experience.

When you feel ready to finish, just come back to your normal state of consciousness.

Sources:

Tantric Vision of the Divine Feminine: The Ten Mahavidyas by David R. Kinsley.

The Sinister Path, Volume 2 by Magan.

Thantifaxath:
A Recollection

Albert Petersen

In 2004 I was offered the opportunity to bear witness to a magickal ritual of a group working in London, England. I was invited to attend the event not as a participant but as an outside observer. Having a profound interest in the occult and also coming from a journalistic background, I jumped at the chance. The following is an extract from a larger body of work currently in development.

I'm not interested in the morals or ethics behind what people choose to do—I usually find any discussions around these areas to be extremely dull and more often than not an indication of deep-seated naiveté. However, I am deeply intrigued by the motivating factors behind a person or group's actions so when, as a result of a casual meeting/conversation in a pub with P (who I later found to be one of the higher ranking priests within the group), I got the offer, I tried to explore as many angles of the event as possible. I have changed names to honour my assurances of confidentiality and admit that much of the following has been rewritten from notes made *in situ*.

As mentioned elsewhere I'm not interested in any particular strain of magick or spirituality; I'll have a crack at most things, incorporating what works for me while dispensing with that which does not yield suitable results. I wouldn't use the word 'tolerant', for this has many negative connotations in my mind. I just let people get on with whatever it is they're doing—as long as it doesn't impinge on me, that's fine. I found several members of the group to have an air of bravado, as if they thought themselves terribly wicked—but through extensive conversations I found them to be relatively 'moral' with the entire group rejecting the use of rape, murder, child-abuse or other nefarious and illegal acts within their rituals. The event took place in an expensive terraced house in Holborn, London where 22 members of the group (I was assured there were several other members who were not required for this particular rite) attempted to communicate with Thantifax-ath, a qliphotic spirit written about extensively in Grant's *Nightside of Eden* and other works.

Two things that struck me immediately was the depth of organisation required for the rite and the sheer number of members of the group. Previous research in this area had yielded only small groups of five or six members, yet here was a large scale occult organisation that somehow managed to circumnavigate the inevitable politics that tend to arise in large groups. Speaking to members after the event, I discovered that each participating member of the rite was allocated a particular task relevant to the ritual. For instance, one person would be responsible for providing the ingredients for the incense, another would be in charge of acquiring appropriate candles and so on. I was most impressed with the degree of organisation and efficiency operating within the group.

The group preferred not to conduct any form of banishing or purification prior to the commencement of the ritual, maintaining that the currents and entities with which they sought communion thrived on 'unclean auras'. Instead all participants fasted for 30 hours prior to the invocation.

As we entered the sitting room, the first thing that struck me was the darkness. Black-out curtains had been pulled across the large bay windows despite the fact that it was three o'clock in the morning. The other thing that struck me was the smell of the incense, which I later recalled as being a mixture of myrrh and sulphur. The smoke from the incense burner was thick and acrid, burning the back of the throat and stinging the eyes and nose; the room was lit by only three tall candles (two black, one dark blue) that sat on what appeared to be a slab of uncarved wood at the back of the room. From my position at the opposite end of the room I could see there was no furniture so I presumed this had all been removed prior to the ritual.

What I did find slightly disconcerting was the fact that there was a metal dish on the altar containing what I can only presume was a large piece of human excrement. I never found out the exact purpose of this, but I presume it was there to throw the participants minds into a state of confusion and repulsion. If that was the desired effect, it was certainly working on me.

Twenty-two members of the group entered the room, all dressed in robes of black, blue and dark purple. A circle was formed consisting of thirteen men and women in robes while the remaining nine members disrobed and formed a square of three rows within the circle. In a solemn manner they all consumed what was termed the 'Wine of the Sabbath'—I was not invited to participate in the sacrament. I later found out the wine consisted of red wine, menstrual/vaginal secretions, semen, black pepper, juniper—and possibly some form of hallucinogen, though no one would confirm this last ingredient.

According to P, the rite technically began at 3:00 a.m. though speaking to interviewees afterwards, I was informed that the ritual truly began at the start of the fasting, which occurred 30 hours beforehand. Despite being in a darkened room, I began to notice imagery that decorated the temple; this included a large double-Tau, flowers (which appeared to be poppies) and crude representations of scorpions, goats and crocodiles. Thantifaxath's sigil took pride of place on the altar, which I also noted to be strewn with oyster shells. Again, later I found the shells to be from the last thing eaten before fasting began.

The group took up a chant of ABAB AGIEL ZAZEL ARANTHRON, and it was at this point that I realised that the majority of correspondences used were those traditionally allocated to Binah. The chanting was quite beautiful with distinct layers to it; for instance one section was repeating ABAB. AB. ABA. ABAB in a low tone while another group was powerfully vocalising AG. AGIEL. AGIEL ZAZEL, and so forth. The many different syllables filled the room in a weird harmony. When questioning members after the event, I found that there were no hard and fast rules regarding who sang what. Each participant knew the chants appropriate to the ritual and went with what seemed right. The chanting got very loud and I wondered if there were neighbours who might call the police. By now I was feeling kind of nauseous—from the incense I presumed—and I also felt slightly anxious, though I could not pinpoint exactly why, as I have been a witness and a participant in many rituals. There was a distinct sensation of rising panic which I strove to throw off.

The circle of thirteen began to adopt what I can only describe as 'whole of body mudras', alternating between right arm down with the left arm extended at a forty-five degree angle from the waist, and another pose with both arms held up, the hands at shoulder height. The 'square' inside the circle did not adopt these mudras.

The chanting continued for what seemed like hours, and despite being an outside observer, I began to feel the effects of the work; the anxiety had been replaced with a sense of claustrophobia, and there were moments when I seriously felt that I was going to choke. I wanted to leave but knew that as a professional, it was impossible for me to do so. I fought back the panic and tried to focus on recording what was occurring in the temple.

I'm not sure at what point the following began as I'd been distracted by analysing my own physical well-being, but when I returned my attention to the group, I noticed that the naked participants of the 'square' were rocking back and forth, some on their haunches, some standing, a few in the traditional lotus position. It later transpired that those in the square formation were deemed 'The Potentialities' and were given almost free reign (aside from breaking the circle) to do whatever seemed suitable to invoke the spirit.

I noticed that at no point was the name Thantifaxath spoken, though I did note that all nine members in the square were also decorated with the appropriate sigil, which was painted on their naked torsos in what looked like river mud. I remember thinking at the time that I thought this extremely unwise. Another clear memory of the night was the thought "Is it any wonder that people think you're Satanists when you're mucking around with shit and blood and god knows what?" though as far as I knew P and the group were in no way associated with Devil-Worship.

Candlemass by Isabel gaborit

By now my whole body was aching painfully. My muscles were stiff and I desperately wanted to sit down; however, I had agreed to stand quietly and not get in the way or distract the group. I just wanted to leave. Again I began introspecting but this time I 'caught myself' before I became too distracted and returned my focus to what was occurring in the room. The naked members were performing sexual acts on themselves including masturbation, the insertion of what looked like soapstone effigies of various totems into their vaginas and anuses, removing said effigies and sucking on them and wiping them across their bodies. Strange patterns (possibly other sigils?) that I did not recognise were drawn on the skin, leaving glittering trails of saliva and secretions on numerous bodies. I could imagine that to an outsider not familiar with such rites it would have been simultaneously strange, repulsive and bizarrely erotic. For me there was a sexual element to it, but I was more intrigued from an anthropological perspective. I was keen to see what would happen next, though I will admit that the introduction of the sexual aspect to the rite renewed my interest and I temporarily forgot about my physical discomfort.

I sensed we were approaching the peak of the rite as the nine persons in the circle began to utter forth the following; in some instances one person would start a sentence or speak only one word while another would pick up the remaining portion of the sentence. The following has been transcribed as a continuous monologue though it was actually spoken by several members:

"Aossic, you cunt…shoving coke in the priestess's cunt…you cunt…I see you…back in time…with your fucking fictions…there is no occult secret…give it up…too much emphasis on one life alone? One book alone…" The speech was interrupted by bouts of laughing, wailing, etc. "Your memories are not divine…getting off on watching witches piss…that's what you're all doing. Hiding your lust in laughably noble magic…you play at magic. Play at magic. Play at magic. Hiding your dirty lust in robes and books. Take a fresh page, throw stars down, recognise the sigil for its worth and function. Intuit and believe. Kadaf (Kadath?), kadosh, kaph. Choose it and chew it. You have set a fool on the throne and will weep for your errors. Stupid, stupid, stupid (this spoken quite tearfully, accompanied by a shaking of the head). You need a new direction, a new erection. Lacking originality, you make tenuous connections with fictions. Fucking fictions. I, the nameless, I, the void, have been, am and will be, always, all ways. You are obsessed—and with wrongness you run in wrongness, wrongness, wrong directions. Wrong erections.

Thantifaxath: A Recollection

Leap, leap ever higher…the coffin is empty for the corpse has leapt and left… the word is the phallus and you will choke on the word. It will stick in your throat like the apple in the first son's neck. Pan is all. The innocent dragged into the web, a sacrifice of circumstance.

"Long and wide, time is cast aside as you…you…you are stretched like fine wire beyond yourself. You cunt…the eye will burn from this sun…" At this point one of the oracles fixed their gaze on a particular member of the circle. "So you want a crystal, aye? Eye. It is done. Now worship me for my kindness or fall foul of my fetid breath that burns the field in the noon-day heat. The king is buried in a pauper's grave and you have stolen the word from his mouth, supplanting it with your very own fingers. Make it thus. Make it thus. Make it thus. Many, many, many, many, many, many times. The density chokes, push onward, upward. No tricks, no numbers. Onward, onward. How to honour thee? With blood and flowers and copulations. Fuck, fuck, fuck, fuck, fuck, fuck, fuck. You'll learn. You'll keep." These last two words were spoken in a disturbingly harsh tone and have stuck in my memory almost more than anything else. This speech probably took approximately 15 to 20 minutes from start to finish.

At the point when the last words were uttered, the nine almost simultaneously dropped to the floor and appeared to be quite comatose. It was quite an effect. The rest of the group performed the necessary closing of the temple, this was despite the fact that no purification/opening rituals were conducted. The nine were then attended to by the other members of the group who supplied them with hot towels, blankets and the like.

Personally I have my own doubts as to whether contact was made (thereby being a true manifestation) or if it were a subconsciously streamed release from the oracles/members desire to redirect the group's energies, or if this were some sort of coup to overthrow the group's current organizational structure. I did hear from one member that there were several people in the group who felt they were heading "down a wrong path; a dead-end," which raised my suspicions further regarding the received communication. Was this an attempt to subtly direct the group in a new direction? At the time of commencing the ritual, I learned that they were all highly respectful of Grant's work, and it would have been bordering on blasphemy to openly suggest that Grant may have perhaps been heading in the wrong direction.

Some weeks later I discovered that a crystal had been 'discovered' by one of the members present on that night; as it turns out they previously expressed a desire for a new scrying crystal some months earlier but had been unable to find a satisfactory one. I say 'discovered' but the crystal was actually 'found' and purchased from a stall in Camden Market; apparently it was exactly what the member had been looking for. Many of the group took this as a confirmation that the invocation had been a success.

I have kept in touch with P and the group for many years since and have extensive field notes from other work that they undertook (with myself either as a participant or as an observer) that I am currently working on as part of a larger project.

THE ORACLE OF THE VOID
(Amprodias Exploration in the 11ᵀᴴ Tunnel)

Edgar Kerval

...Transcending the purple veil,
Burning the incense of human flesh,
Rising the throne of bones,
And chanting through the palace of madness...

Amprodias is the messenger that rambles through the tunnels as an oracle of the void, spreading the secret wisdom related with divination, writtings, and the artistic creative nature. The sinister rays from its uterus engender powerful seeds of wisdom, intuition and intelligence. Amprodias guides us through the mysteries of transformation from men-beast from its uterus, giving birth to the shadows of the void. Its spectrum is the ones of the void itself and its manifestations occur mapping its secrets routes via the hidden light of its own ascending through the labyrinths.

On the path of Amprodias we work with primal darkness, focusing this as an integral part of our consciousness, creating an infernal union that guides us to an inner awareness and the development of ecstasies of the primal qliphotic mysteries beyond the tunnel itself, adapting the forms of Amprodias not as a living entity separated from yourself, but as a primigenian abortion of the gnosis of madness and pain made manifest though yourself, a process of the magickal formula of annihilation, born and dying as a god in the tunnels all the time, and reflecting this in this existential plane.

As a servant of the primigenian void, Amprodias rises as a great purple hole full of thorns opening a magickal vortex to the influx of diverse trans-human entities, extending consciousness into other realities inside the tunnels or astral labyrinths. Amprodias as a master of divination floats through vast primordial memories in men, as a suggestive power to align the labyrinth maps under diverse paths, formed by ophidian stones and abstract forms appearing as a primigenian purple fire and vaporous putrescence.

Transcending the sempiternal void under Amprodias awakens and develops all its primal atavistic powers into this life. And is through its sacred tendrils and transformative masks when hidden gnosis emerge giving us its powers, attributes and abilities.

THE RITE OF ISOLATED FLAME OF BLINDING MADNESS

The following ritual is designed according to personal purposes within the mysterious union with Amprodias and its essential forces, which are rotted to subconscious realms. Through a correct use of this one you shall burn inside you the flame of isolation, reflecting the deep void in which Amprodias and you shall be submerged as a sole union rising from a vast black nothingness, offering its marvelous treasures and chaotic wisdom beyond the palace of madness and understanding.

Amprodias Sigil by edgar kerval

To begin with these powerful rituals just take some hours for meditation and self-study of each one of the attributes you want to awake in yourself through the Ambrosias flame. Relax all your body, and when you feel it's a proper moment, just stand up, close your eyes, put on a black tape around

The Oracle Of The Void (Amprodias Exploration in the 11th Tunnel)

your eyes and start moving slowly in spiral again and again. Start visualizing the Amprodias sigil in purple, shining and moving around yourself following the rhythmic pattern of the spiral, creating a purple aura around the tunnel created by the spiral, and continue the visualization until you feel how the floor of the ritual chamber is opening a deep void that devours you slowly.

The Amprodias' tendrils rise from the void itself and carry you to the deep of its primigenian caves; once there you must let the energy invade your body, mind and spirit and the secret oracles manifesting its mysterious and enigmatic wisdom with no restriction. It is very important to feel and obsess yourself with the dynamism and in deep messages manifested by Amprodias, because these are secret formulas which can help you in the exteriorization of its dark energy in all your being and at the same time the transformation of your psyche touching you in an infinite madness. Blindness transcendence as a way of interaction between Amprodias and you. Now the rite is complete; you can feel the tension and energy for some days or even weeks depending on how strong you have been working in this tunnel.

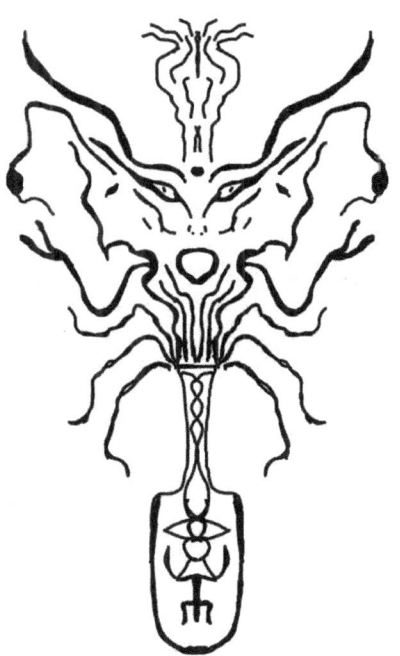

Amprodias Rising by edgar Kerval

Untitled by Barry willliam Hale

Ignition Of The Black Flame

David Eosphorus Maples

A Tiny Introduction

My first steps onto the Vodoun grid were taken on a hot summer night while vacationing in Puerto Rico. I sat pondering the words spoken to me 3 days prior—that the spirits of this ancient religion had been surrounding me since birth and had been awaiting my germination into the spiritual arts. This time had come. I had two choices: accept my spiritual birthright, or deny it and have those gates close to me forever. Endless are the prices for true power. Plenty of (purported) historical facts and theories about Vodoun have surfaced in our present age.

It is beyond the scope of this book and the will of the author to focus on this subject matter. The goal of this work is to spread the Black Flames to the hungry few. Application (Black Flame) is the only law, power and authority. And it is this spiritual authority that will be awakened in those willing to step onto the grid of power.

The Loa and rituals that are presented in this work will be left uncensored and free of unnecessary dogma. They will all be taxing and require the greatest oaths and sacrifices, as the sorcerer will be forced to explore the self and move into areas that are completely uncomfortable and/or paradigm-shattering. As these words are read, and these works performed, you will have become a veritable Black God in your own right.

The Grid

Your first steps into the spirit world are perhaps the most crucial. Great respect and humility is to be maintained when working with Loa, anything less will result in negative backlashes... sometimes literally; these spirits are ancient and harsh. The only way to reap any benefit of working with the Loa is to become a co-conspirator in their master plan.

An altar must be either constructed or bought. Pretty much anything wood or stone that in your mind represents a suitable altar will do just fine. The aesthetics aren't important, that it symbolizes your union with the spirits is all that is necessary. You don't need to burden yourself with trinkets and oddities to place on this altar, as the spirits will provide you with all that is needed.

It has been recommended that this altar be set up in a room other than the bedroom, as many spirits, some potentially harmful, are attracted to the sexual energies that are typically built up in this room. It is left up to the discretion of the reader to decide whether to heed such warnings.

The Rite of Return

[Materials: 8 black tea light candles, 8 white tea light candles, 2 small jars, water, cornmeal or flour (the veve can be drawn on paper using a marker), rum or whiskey.]

The altar should face south. A red, black or purple cloth should cover the altar. Nothing is to be on its top, except for 8 black candles and 8 white candles, in a star arrangement (like an 'x' with a '+' overlaid) in the altar's center. At 10:00 p.m. the candles will be lit and left to burn for the whole 10th hour (or 10 minutes).

After this seemingly obscure and simple candle-lighting ritual, Legba is to be called. The veve will be laid out in cornmeal or drawn on parchment and placed in the middle of the star arrangement. Next, a personally created esoteric prayer is to be said, asking Legba to open up the altar as the crossroads.

After the rapture of this gate-opening has subsided and Legba has given his blessing and scarred you, feed the altar by sprinkling whiskey on it and leaving 2 jars of water, one on each side.

Now immediately draw or lay out Baron Samedi's veve and call out to him. The room will immediately become full of power and death energy. Samedi will attack you for disturbing the dead. Take your punishment and then apologize, asking that he accept you into his mysteries. He may require a sacrifice of extreme obscurity in order to be persuaded. No matter the cost, perform the sacrifice(s) and dance counterclockwise, for the rewards are great for any willing to dive into this current head-first. The spirits are then thanked.

Note: This rite acts as an astral initiation in the Mysteries. A physical ritual will have to take place at some point, but the Loa will allow you glimpses into Guinea and many other worlds even with such a rite as the one above. There are many more portals that will open as we establish our esoteric web of power. Reverence and respect must be maintained at all times, even amongst one another. Take note of the power and presence the jars of water will accumulate.

The Loa have now made that power spot their home, and your home their temple. It is advised that the practitioner quickly become acquainted with the idea that they are no longer in charge of many aspects of their life. Many obstacles and questions can be overcome by simply letting go. The consequences of disobeying and disrespecting the spirits are crass and explicit; the student will learn horrors beyond the fear of their own mortality in those moments.

The idea(s) of what an initiation truly is and what an initiation is supposed to entail has been perverted beyond comprehension. The truth is much deeper than any outsider could ever understand, and infinitely more simple. The powers (Loa, elementals, shades, etc.) will always recognize power—a dark light only radiated by those chosen few who are called to walk the merciless path. Is it then safe to assume that true initiation only comes at the hand of the Loas' meat puppets (priests and priestesses)?

Absolutely not. Admittedly, the relationship of master and student is an indescribably grand luxury, but such physical luxuries only serve as temporal affirmations of the greater truth.

The Dance Of Death

This working is best performed on a Saturday at 11:00, leading into midnight: [Materials: A small wooden box, candy, a photograph of yourself, small toys and rum]

Stand in the middle of the Homfort, facing the south wall. In the wooden box place the candy, photograph and small toy. You may intuitively feel that other ingredients and/or fluids should be added to the box.

Note: My personal Voudon heart contained candy, the photograph, a small toy, blood, semen, a chicken's head and talon, and a fresh rose (as this box is symbolic of the sacred heart of the Black Madonna). Marassa's veve was then engraved on top.

It is important that this intuition is listened to, as it is a direct message from the Loa that guide us. Place this box on the floor. Using esoteric prayer the sorcerer will petition Legba to blanket the Homfort with his presence and energies. The rum is sprinkled over the closed box and Legba is then pleaded with to open the gateway to the realm of shades, to contact Baron Samedi. This initial contact will be very unpleasant and frightening, instilling much humility, but should be continued through until its completion. Draw the veve of Baron Samedi and open it with intent.

Watch and feel as the winds of death enter the Homfort, bringing with them the restless shades and the dreaded Baron. It is at this point that the sorcerer will speak his desires of power to the Baron. Samedi will make his full presence known as he violently mounts the sorcerer, fusing life and death (Forbidden Alchemy). When mounted, the sorcerer will see through Samedi's eyes the legions of shades at his disposal—it is this power we have come to contract Baron for.

Through a furious dance of movements and spoken words the secrets of summoning the shades will be revealed. It is best that all of this and any other experiences be recorded in a journal immediately following the ritual's conclusion and meditated upon. The Baron may then speak and/or act through the sorcerer, revealing further instructions and secrets of the dead.

After Samedi has taken his leave, call out again to Legba and ask him to open the wooden box (which is just a symbolic representation of the core of the sorcerer) as a cross-lattice in the spirit grid. The veve of Kalfu is then laid out, and the box left in its center. Kalfu is then too called down to open the box as a backdoor. Maintain utmost respect (he will accept nothing less) as he comes and thank him for answering your call. Speak your desire and leave the room as Kalfu does his infernal workings. It is not uncommon to hear many thuds and bangs around the house and Homfort as Kalfu works.

The spirits are then thanked and fed. All experiences are recorded. The box can be buried at a crossroad, or left in a place with constant sunlight during the day and covered with a black cloth at sunset (later we will have a special place for this box, which is the Voudon heart). This ritual acts to birth both the positive and negative solar powers in the sorcerer.

There are many who are of the opinion that such self(ish) initiation rites and secrets are without merit and inherently dangerous. Their opinions do not matter. The Loa are ancient, powerful and wise, more than capable of spotting the true Brothers of the Black Flame and the charlatan(s).

*Veve of Legba
by edgar kerval*

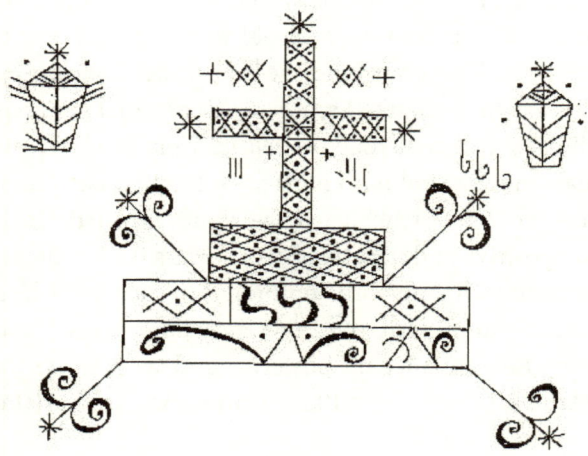

Veve of Baron Samedi

*Veve of Kalfu
by edgar kerval*

Workings with Kalfu are the most secular and evil. Kalfu is the Voudon god of all black magicks and chaos, and gatekeeper of the hidden off-point directions. This evil god demands absolute respect and fear; he has been known to implant demons and create chaos. Legba, on the other hand, is the Voudon god of the Sun, opener and closer of gateways, the cardinal directions and the crossroads.

As such, he is also the remover and placer of obstacles and doors, infinitely powerful, wise and deviant. Take great care in workings with this trickster. Baron Samedi is the Voudon god of Death. He is the master of all cemeteries and shades. Samedi is also the master of divinations, black magicks and life—housing both the powers of the heavens and the hells.

The above given veves can be used for a multitude of powerful workings, but it is best that the sorcerer discover each of the Loa's hidden signatures. These secret veve signatures provide a map of their terrain on the Voudon grid, and are acquired as you increase your workings with the Loa. These keys provide secret accesses to initiation, revelation and hidden magicks. One such forbidden ritual came from Kalfu. He called this evil spell 'Drinking the Soul'.

Drinking the Soul

[Materials: cornmeal, black and red candles, rum with hot peppers in it]

Arrange and light all of the red and black candles you brought for this ritual. Lay down Kalfu's veve while mentally calling out for him to hear your plea. You will ask that he allow you to possess the form of a mosquito. When you have finished the veve, take the rum that is infused with hot peppers (Kalfu says that this is a sacrilegious act since rum is a sacred drink) and sprinkle a hefty amount on the open veve, vocalizing your call to the black god Kalfu. His coming will be furious and frenzied, bringing with it the most evil and demonic of Loas. Submit to Kalfu immediately and show respect, or face torture and death. He will know why you have called for his arrival and he will have his decision.

> *Please Note: Kalfu is very harsh and may require you to work with him many times before granting you such a request, if he would ever grant such a request. The inner teachings of Kalfu are the true teachings of the most evil and vile magicks.*

Qliphoth Opus III

Zobop Mosquito

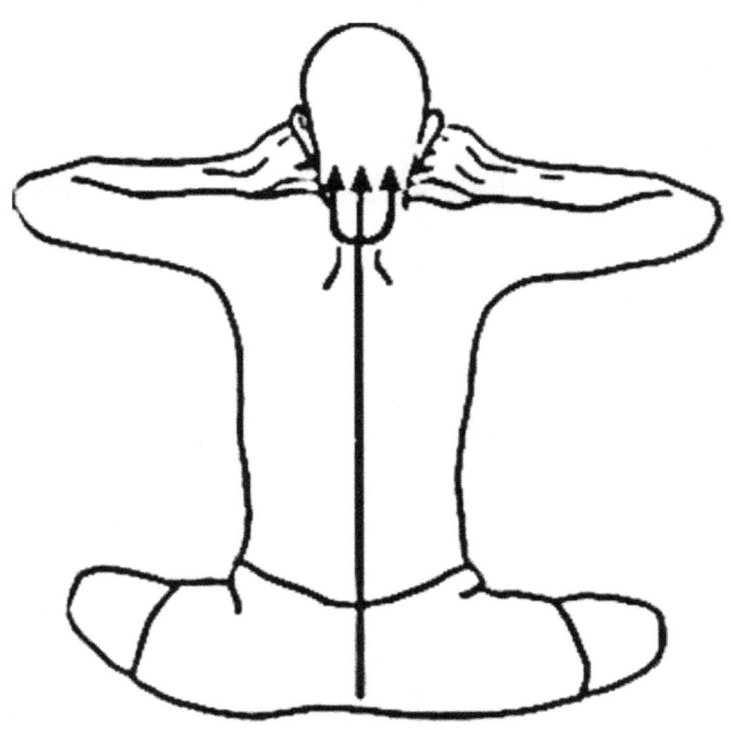

Bindu Trident

Once you have possession of the astral mosquito form, seek out your target. Once the target has been found, drink from the top back of their head. This spot on the body has been known to possess the lunar nectar of life. If the sorcerer drinks of another person's life force, then he will be shortening the victim's life span while increasing his own. Such an act is truly vampiric and evil, the nature of Kalfu.

Return to your body now and thank Kalfu for allowing such a powerful magick to be performed. In time, such dark magicks will be performed through simple acts, such as gesturing, touching and suggestion. Drench the Homfort entirely with the remaining hot rum, allowing Kalfu and his evil to feed and grow.

After these and any additional workings the Loa may have you do, prepare a small table to become the personal altar of the Black Madonna. This altar should be covered with a red cloth. This altar will hold any images or statues you may have found representative of Erzuli Dantor—she who guides and protects all of the Loa's children. Around these images should remain flowers and perfumes of the

most beautiful and pleasant nature. The Voudon heart created in your earlier working is to be placed on this altar, left in the sunlight of the day and covered with a black cloth at night. Using her veve, call down Erzuie Dantor and ask that she guide and protect your physical and spiritual life. Blessings upon you and your work, sorcerer!

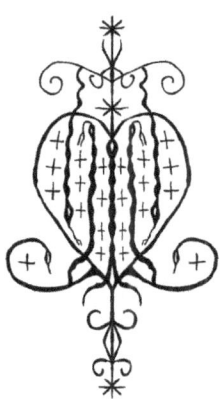

Veve of Erzuli Dantor
by edgar kerval

©David Maples & The Blood Moon Cultus of the Black Madonna

Hell's Rapture

Mica Gries

"And upon her forehead was a name written, MYSTERY, BABYLON THE
GREAT, THE MOTHER OF HARLOTS AND ABOMINATIONS OF THE EARTH."
Revelations 17:5

The shower head explodes. Streams of hot water fly through the air, across the shiny plastic surface, and gurgle helplessly down the drain, into pipes which lead down, down under the earth. A young, naked woman steps into its cascade. The heat at first shocks her, but quickly becomes a welcome embrace. Pale, supple skin slides over itself, cleans itself in the familiar ritual. Hair is washed, conditioner is applied. Soap is spread across and beneath her arms, on her breasts, between her cheeks, down her legs and on her slender feet. A razor, brand new, slides eagerly across her skin, seeking ingress. First, the legs and underarms are shaved, and then her mound is made smooth and hairless like a young girl. Her body is made clean and shiny, her hourglass figure the sort that masses spend a fortune to attain and sustain.

In eternal midnight, my body is spread across oceans of spit and lust. To you, I give every last drop. I await your call, mistress.

She steps out of the stall, and stands quietly before the mirror for a moment, expressionless. But even without expression, hers is the face that always gleams with the devilish innocence of the young and rebellious. The hair is combed back, and lotion is rubbed into the skin. Every square inch of nerve endings are teased and tickled into excitation. Face cream, deodorant and a light floral water is sprayed across the neck and wrists. Long, dark strands of wet hair sway in the heat of an electric dryer.

There is a pleasing kind of tension in the manipulation of appearance; the private motions we entertain. It is the building up of an image, the building up of a charge—and always with specific intent.

I am wrapped about in a robe of wet dreams. Open, naked mouths. Soft, wet breasts. Every pore of skin is an orifice, against which my robe shudders and squirms. It is my comfort, my sole consolation, while I wait, and when at last I see you again, I shall open my robe to you, and enwrap us both.

Her face is painted now in the colors of the Kama Sutra. Her black miniskirt, knee-high boots and white, almost see-through halter-top display her as a thing of desire. She is ready. She makes her leave. And as she pulls out of the driveway and down the street, a man waiting quietly for her starts his black Mercedes, and follows behind.

The woman owns a red sports car, the kind that makes you wonder what she does for a living. It does not matter, however, because soon she is just one pair of the many thousands of head-lights, cruising along in the after-dark current of metal and exhaust, a teeming mass of purpose and frustration, anticipation and escape. Another street, another summer night in some insignificant American city. The boredom seeps into everyone like a plague, making us do things, become things that are monstrous in their hunger.

Twenty minutes later, she is pulling into a public parking lot. It is 9:32pm, and the dark-skinned man at the booth takes her money and eye-fucks her. She finds a space, and walks the two blocks to what would look like a small warehouse, were it not for the word "Fluid" proclaimed in wavy neon light above the doorway. A line-up for the night club waits outside—a babbling herd of hormones and insecurity, they laugh and shout and sneer. Low, throbbing sexual vibrations pound through the metal and mortar. Standing there, she feels the evening's first ache of longing, rushing up her legs in a tingle. She enters, and is enveloped in a throng of flesh and movement; a room where every shadow tastes like sex. The DJ is good tonight.

A few minutes after, a single middle-aged man enters the club in an expensive suit. He is as out of place as a pin in a pocket, and the surrounding patrons eye him warily. He watches the woman work her way in from the edge of the dance floor, her body lightly swaying. The crowd easily parts, and she catches several eyes like a baited hook dangling by a school of fish. Girls like her get what they want.

At the center of the dance floor, she lets go. The music lifts up her body like a lover, and lets it take control. Her little skirt flying, her schoolgirl tongue licking her schoolgirl mouth, the music fucks her hard, just the way she likes it. The beats, oh God, the beats—each one like a thrust inside her. Here, there are no dancers, only the dance; all writhing blood and bone. Together, as a single pulsing mass, mere meat caresses the threshold of the world.

Soon, she is surrounded by men. She does not worry yet which one she will pick. She lets them flutter around her like moths, casting furtive glances in her direction. She closes her eyes and forgets everything.

And then she feels a hand on her ass. Her eyes open, but she does not immediately turn around. The hand continues down the back of her leg and turns inward to cup her thigh, lightly, suggestively pulling back. It is here she turns her head to the side, glaring behind her, a delicate snarl on her lips. She pushes her ass back, and meets the resistance of the man's jeans. He grins at her behind the large lenses of a pair of aviator sunglasses. He grins at her with cigar and beer breath, a tattooed bicep, and the confidence of a young man who is not used to rejection.

They grind together on the dance floor without shame. One hand on her hip, the other kneading a breast through the fabric, he rides, and she lets herself be ridden. He opens his mouth and howls. A victory! The howl is taken up by others, their bloodlust increased. His prey smiles through her sweat.

She turns around to face him, a half-smile still on her lips, and reaches into her top, between her breasts, to retrieve a small vial. Opening the lid, she sticks her finger in and pulls out a black, oily gob. "What the fuck is that?" he yells to her over the music.

In reply, she leans in close, brings her lips to his ear, and says, "It makes you fuck like a god." His breath sucks in a ragged hiss as she takes her finger in her mouth and

slowly, teasingly sucks off the drug. Dipping in her finger again, she brings the drug close to his lips and says, "Your turn." Her finger enters his mouth and the bitter, musky ooze slides down his throat.

Inevitably, their mouths lock together and her tongue replaces her finger. As his kiss deepens, she opens her eyes, and spies, standing six feet away, an older man in an expensive suit, watching them.

"Let's go," she says after separating. "My place. Just follow behind."

My blood is a river of drowned souls, clamoring for breath. My bones are the fog-covered hills and mountains where lovers weep and dragons roam. My skin is without end, and pierced through with hooks, each one a moment in time, each and every moment filled with you.

Within half an hour, they arrive. There is a wind in the night now, making the trees in the neighborhood wary and restless. The stars shift a little closer to the edge of the sky, watching intently. And not long after they enter the house, a black Mercedes pulls up and stops across the street. The man turns off the car, pulls his cellphone out of a pocket in his coat, and begins to dial. The couple enters and the door closes behind them. He slams her up against the wall, lifts up her skirt and begins to pull down her underwear.

"Not here," she says.

"Right fucking here."

"*No*," she says. "I want to tie you up."

He laughs in her face. "And what if I tie *you* up?"

She smiles. "You first."

He laughs, differently this time; with her, not at her. "Momma, I've caught a wild one."

Her tongue stirs worm-like in her mouth, wanting release. "Take off your shirt," she says.

As he is busy removing his top, she gropes his cock, tenderly at first, and then grabs it like she has a hold of a leash.

"Come, dog!"

"Yes, mistress," he says through a smile.

He notices as he passes through the living that the house seems almost empty. There is furniture, but only the bare minimum, and it doesn't feel lived in. There are no pictures on the walls, and everything is so clean.

everything must die exept my love for you by isabele gaborit

She leads him down the hall, and into a bedroom. Dominating the room is a queen-sized, black, four-poster bed, with leather restraints strapped to each post. On the other side of the room, and the only other piece of furniture, is an enormous, baroque-style, mirrored armoire.

She has him lie down on the bed, restrains his wrists, and with a quiet, almost maternal tenderness, pulls down his jeans and navy blue boxers. Much to his surprise, it is not being undressed by her, but the sound of leather being stretched and tightened that makes him hard. It is the sound of control being surrendered.

She steps away and surveys her catch—his arms and legs spread-eagled, his head propped up with comfy pillows, his phallus quietly crying for attention.

"Do you like what you see, darling?" he asks her. She says nothing, but crosses the room and, turning a key which dangles in the lock, opens the armoire.

A lump of saliva awkwardly catches in his throat. "What the fuck?" he mutters as she attends to the strange, simple altar revealed inside the cabinet. She lights a few candles and incense on a small stand, on which also sits a large antique copper bowl. Pinned to the back wall of the armoire is a canvas adorned in black ink with an odd symbol composed of interlocking v-shaped lines. A bathrobe hangs inside, on a door. She gazes at the symbol for a minute, as he gazes at her back, and she begins to slowly strip off her clothes.

Still turned away from him, she says, "Don't say another motherfucking word."

The darkness crawls across her naked back in patches and bands. The miniskirt falls to the floor. She turns around then, the vial of drug in her hands, and steps toward the bed, her black hair cascading around swelling breasts. She slides onto the foot of the bed and creeps up between his legs, his erection inches from her face. She puts a finger to her lips, "Ssssshhhh…" He does not speak, but his mouth is open and his breath is shallow. She unstops the vial of the drug, pulls out a nice wad of the thick, black sludge and spreads it across his belly in lines and curves. Soon, he can see that same symbol from the cabinet smeared across his own flesh.

She pulls her face forward, and he thinks he will finally get his reward for his patience and his duty. Instead, she bends her lips down to the symbol, and kisses the v of the arrow, his cock nestled in the crook of her neck.

Hell's Rapture

She whispers a poem to the black rune:

> "You whom the earth reviles
> You whom the stars fear
> You whose voice drives out the light
> I call you.
> You whom the aeons cannot touch
> You whom the owls adore
> You whose countenance is legion
> I call you.
>
> I call you from your throne of night
> I call you from stone, I call you from blood
> I call you from the lust of men
> I call you
>
> Samael, Samael, Samael…"

She continues to repeat the name, over and over and over again. Her head lifts up, sphinx-like, to gaze upon the inside of her skull, palms pressed into the mattress on either side of him. Smoke from the incense fills the room and is caught up in the light of the candles, swirling in patterns dictated by her breath.

Upon the first utterance of the name, the man feels a clawing in the air, as of something pressing against it. To his disappointment, he finds all manhood has fled from him. He decides he does not want to play this game anymore. The air begins to close around him, and he finds himself sweating uncomfortably. But he is suddenly too afraid of her to speak. This, however, he does not think aloud. He would not admit to himself his underlying fear of the female body, driving him to conquer it.

"Samael, Samael, Samael…" she continues, ceaselessly, the name dribbling from her lips like the mumbling of a sleepwalker. In the half-sleep of her trance, the room is no more. Each handful of space trembles with infinity, with absolute possibility. The incense smoke, now choking the air, weaves between the worlds. Through that void, she feels the familiar pressure, some *thing* brushing up against the substance of her mind, responding to her summons. She knows its presence; she welcomes it.

"Samael, Samael, Samael..."

"Shut up! Shut up!" he shouts at her, but only in his head. To his confusion, no words form on his lips. He struggles against the leather restraints, but only in his mind. His limbs refuse to listen. That is when the panic starts.

Yes, my mistress, I come.

Her voice increases in speed and volume, the very atoms of the smoke throbbing to her voice. The smoke congeals and wraps itself together, slowly spinning upon an unseen axis above the bed; a whirling dust-devil whose tip rests upon the man's belly, its maw opening to the worlds beyond worlds. The man's eyes are shrieking wide like a frightened horse, the rest of his flesh paralyzed by the entity.

"Samael! Samael! Samael!" The vortex spins faster and faster, a tornado of smoke, matching the violence of her now shrieking voice. The very blood inside the man's head screams, and he suddenly remembers, with vivid clarity, that he only screamed like this once before: as he was being born. And that is his last thought.

It descends. The witch-light burns in its fall, an emerald jewel from the crown of hell.

A silence covers the room, heavier than the smoke, and breaks it apart with deadly grace. But the silence too is quickly dispatched. A low, tortured, bull-like moan breaks out from the man's throat, a sound that should not come from a man. The moan becomes a wail, and his body begins to shake. The body's primordial intelligence—every last cell—fights against the invading spirit. But she is prepared for this. She is already straddling the body—a writhing leather-bound slab of meat—and feels his cock swell against her thigh.

And this is when the drug kicks in.

She rises off him and, pressing down on his thighs to keep him still, peers down at his organ, like she's never seen one before. The thing is huge, angry and red—the color of a disemboweled and throbbing intestine, squirming of its own accord, more like a hungry maggot than anything else. Her tongue creeps out and she takes a long, slow lick from balls to head, the mouth of the urethra opening and closing as saliva drips down its throat. Like an angry sea suddenly finding peace, the body comes to a rest, and the wailing becomes merely the low, heavy breathing of a man.

And then a whisper, barely heard: "Release me."

She cannot help but tremble as her hands reach for the restraints, the leather falling open. The beast waits patiently, staring into space, until all four limbs are free. And then he falls on her like a shower of meteors out of the night sky.

Have you ever seen the fornication of eagles? With talons clasped, they fall with grace, as full of pleasure as the nearness of death upon their tender impact. With eyes rolled back, our woman, our priestess, our temple whore, she rehearses her embrace of death; not, as before, with the hard, hot beats of the rave, but with the sound of hissing insects and the hollow heartbeat of another, darker world.

With the drug in her brain and the sex between her legs, a new world opens up before her, sharp and full of the light of unknown stars. The light comes out in words and images of indefinable beauty; words she hears from the mouth of her lover.

"When you're in my arms, mistress, my body is a stone that watches you with dark marbles of saliva. I watch you bleed like your dreams, the hard rock floor sucking at your doe-flesh. I watch you scream like the cat you are, ringing the moon out of your hair."

The unholy starlight pours from out her cunt and erects cathedrals in which the chosen are baptized in the semen of the black sun. Her skull is pried open, to drink freely the oceans of promise.

"All who drink of me shall know me. And I give you every last drop. Drink it all, my mistress. Drink every last drop."

He says this as he stands over her, his cock spewing a black viscous oil into the copper bowl which she holds out before her reverently. The oil pours and pours, a steady stream, draining the body of its strength and vitality. The beast reaches out to touch her once more, straining against its failing reserves. The black suddenly gives way to red as blood is pissed out the genitals. She pulls the bowl away and watches as his knees give out and slumps to the floor. She stands up, places the now full bowl on the altar and stands over the prostrate form, still bleeding a little from his sex. He looks at her with fading eyes. She looks back at him, and says a single word, "Goodnight."

And then he is gone. The shattered remnant of the human soul remains, twitching and gasping and drooling across the floor. She watches this with a smile, before donning the bathrobe from the cabinet, crossing the room, and opening the door.

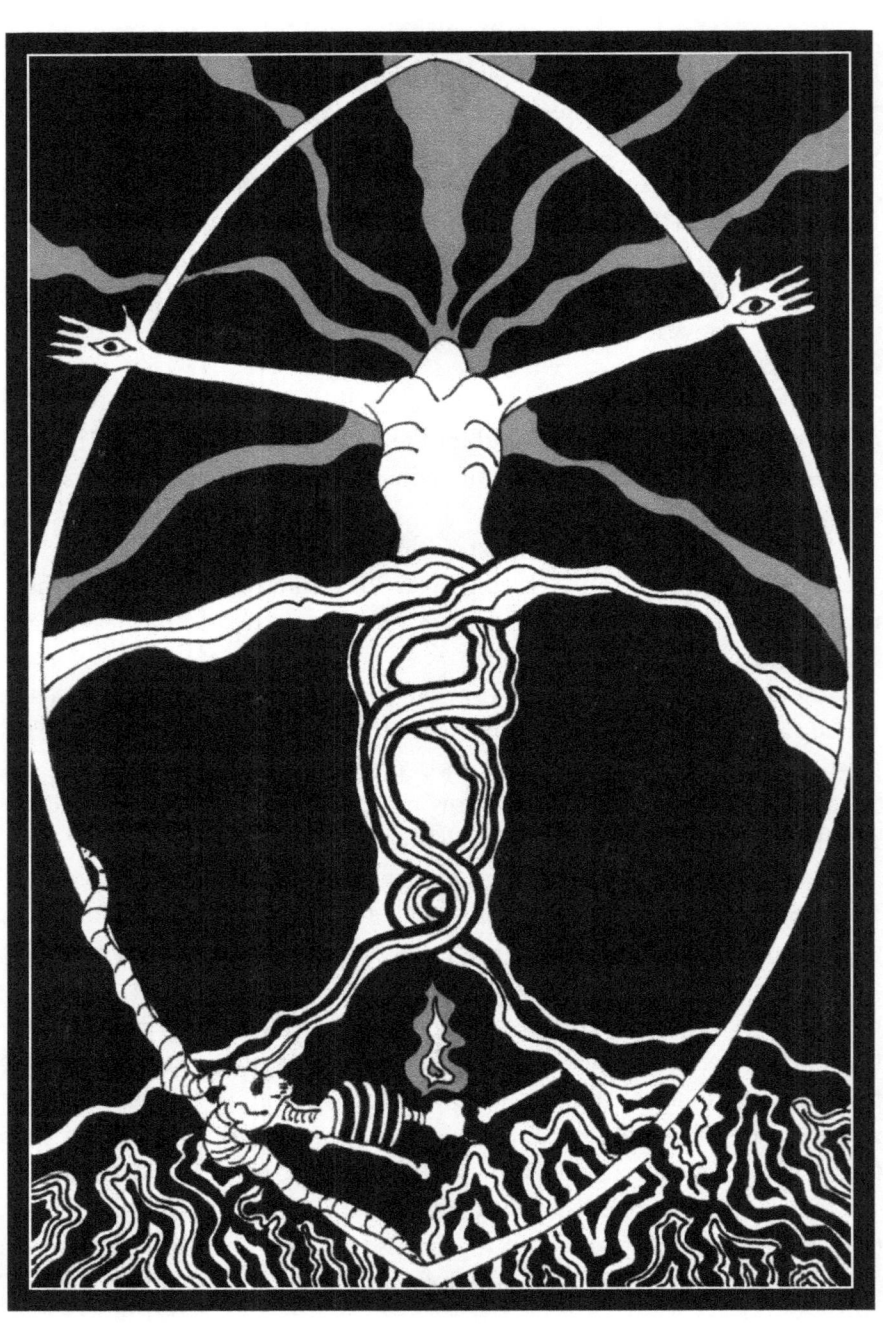

from the bonefire of our love by isabele gaborit

The man in the suit is waiting for her on the other side. She nods her head, and two young men—thugs—enter the room behind her: the clean-up crew. The man in the suit walks toward the kitchen and she follows behind him, the sound of a muffled gunshot ringing through the house. They sit in folding chairs beside a table on which sits a pen, paper, a spoon, a thermometer, a funnel and a two-liter graduated cylinder. One of the men suddenly returns, bearing the copper bowl, careful not to spill a single drop.

The man in the suit takes the spoon and stirs the ooze, before holding the thermometer in the bowl for thirty seconds. He notes the temperature on the paper, and then asks the woman to hold the funnel as he pours the bowl's contents in the cylinder. They both stare at the little measuring lines on the glass.

He turns to her and speaks. "1.35 liters. The market price has risen 20%, so your cut will be 10% more. As agreed, we will handle the disposal of evidence, for the usual fee. Is this satisfactory?"

"Yes."

"Good. There is a suitcase by the door, containing one-hundred fifty thousand dollars, in hundred dollar bills. The rest will be delivered to you in a week."

She gets up, leaves the house, and returns to her car, suitcase in hand. As she drives home, still dressed in nothing but her blue silk robe, she thinks about how all the things we cannot see or hear—the things our parents told us do not exist—outnumber us in numbers we cannot fathom. She thinks about how a little insect, as it is consumed by a bird or a bat, cannot fathom the existence of its predator. So too are we food for things we cannot imagine, as are they, too, only part of the vast web of life and death. There is nothing alive or otherwise that sits atop the food chain.

Her red sports car merges with the current on the freeway, and with all the lights of the city. Above, the stars watch, and wait.

By Mica Gries

666+156=93 by rafal kosela

Ielejkjn Heleikinn– Necromancy

Ljóssál Loðursson

The term used to define Necromancy within the Þursatrú Seiðr context has been coined by Vexior as "Heleikinn". A compound word that describes the knowledge that death can bring. The first part of the word is "Hel", the Gýgr which rules all of the Heldrasil; the second part of the word is "Leikin", one of the names of this Gýgr, it represents her destructive aspect and the splendor of her baleful sorcery. The final term is "Kinn", whose root is "Kyn" (lineage) and refers to the transfer of sacred forces through bloodlink. The practice and knowledge developed through necromantic techniques is not limited to Evocations or Invocations of those who no longer have Önd, the Breath of Life. There are several disciplines that can be derived from this branch of the art, and each of these can show us how to achieve control or command over the forces that surround us. In this chapter I will detail two practices that can be useful for the Black Arts practitioner: The Spectrum's Whisper and The Corpse's Whisper. Trying to explain Heleikinn's nature in such a short text would not be able to do justice to a knowledge that can take one or more rebirths to be fully understood.

I will limit myself to these two aspects of the Tree of Death, the contact with different beings that can be found in the Heldrasil and the mysteries found in the mystical dissection.

In Heleikinn, as in the rest of the Þursatrú Seiðr, we must create a Varð Lokkur according to the type of intent that we want to express. We must be ever vigilant because the previously mentioned elements that we have used to perform our magical song do not work in this art. This procedure is linked to the forces of death and implies that the operational process changes its structure in a subtle but important way.

Kvisanár – The Corpse's Whisper

This mystery is linked to the Like or physical body. Unlike traditional Seiðr in Necromancy we find that the elements of Nature do not play a central role, rather we address the root from which they appear. A clue related to this process can be seen in Ymir's dissection, the Corpse of the Son of Chaos. Every corpse is infested with Ymir's essence. If we have the opportunity to work with a dead body, we can use it to create potential changes in the universe. Each of the Acasual body parts of Ymir was employed in the Creation of Yggdrasil, this act empowered all the characteristics of our plane of existence. Therefore, through experiments with each body part of the corpse of the first Hrimþursar we can rule all forces of Nature or another living being as such. This practice requires great understanding and sincere passion for these practices. It should not be done by those who are unfamiliar with funeral and burial processes.

Should the practitioner get a corpse (be it fresh, decomposing or bones only) each body part can serve as a channel to tame or subdue the kingdom of life using energies from the kingdom of death thereby achieving control over all that Óðinn created using the body of the first chaotic Ice Giant.

Controlling a human being: The procedure is essentially simple. Take a body part that you think might be helpful to your cause, one that relates to the aspect that you want to control in the victim. Proceed to carve your purpose in runes, weave the spell using black heart runes and nightside runes. Do not forget to carve the name of the person you want under your control; if you cannot write upon the body part, then whisper your intentions over the same.

The Varð Lokkur songs used during Necromancy practices should be whispered because the dead do not produce any sound, and when they do, they emit it softly to our ears. Examine the following table carefully and perform the chant related to the specific body part while visualizing how the energy is transferred from the corpse's body part to the victim's body part. This Chthonic energy transfer generates a link or direct connection between the Draugr (corpse ghost) and the victim.

Body	Hármál	To control
Flesh	Slátr	Instinct
Bones	Bein	Will
Blood	Dreyri	Emotions
Teeth	Tonn	Words
Hair	Skör	Appearance
Worms	Ormr	Energy
Cranium	Hauss	Memory
Skull	Heili	Thoughts
Sparks	Sparkr	Spirit

As the practitioner continuously whispers the Varð Lokkur, allow the Óður to flow completely while maintaining a complete visualization of energy transfer; this kind of practice requires a powerful trance since controlling the forces of death involves a powerful Hamingja discharge.

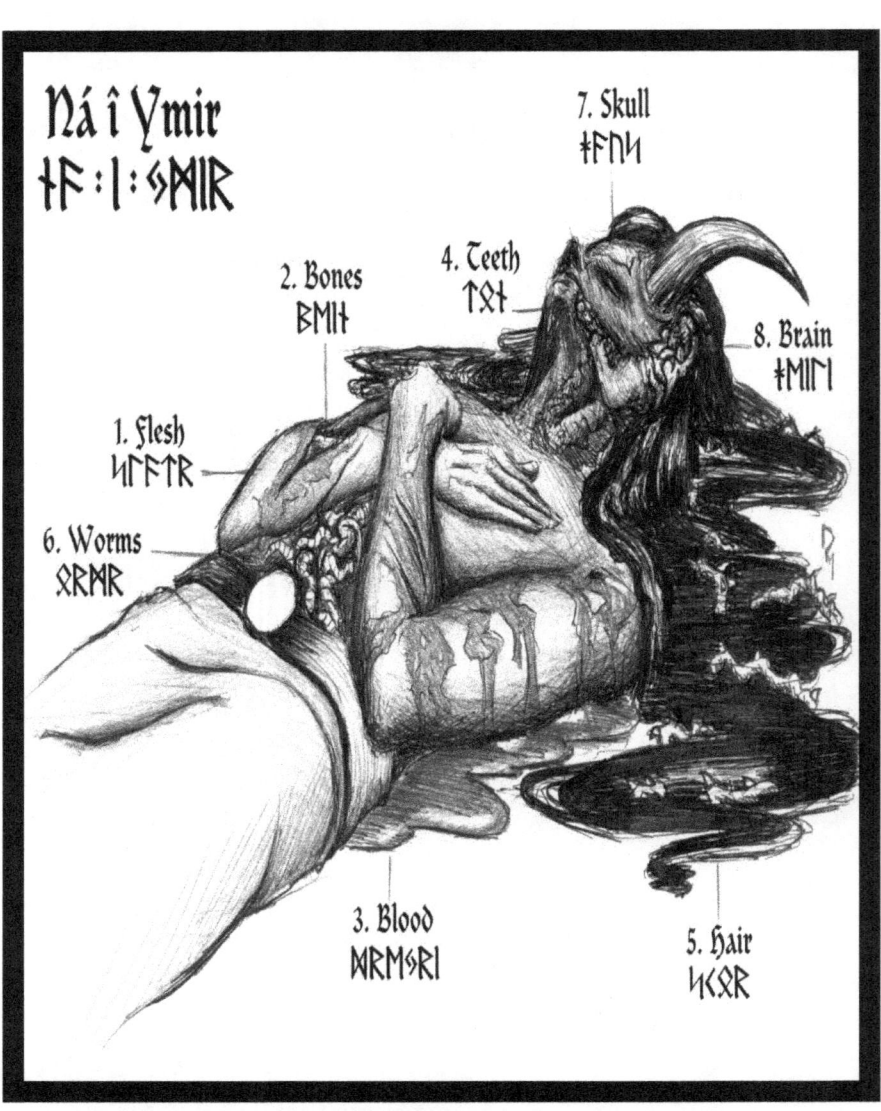

Heleikinn– Necromancy....... Ljóssál Loðursson

When the *Óður* has descended, do not banish or encircle in order to keep the mortuary energies active after the ritual, proceed to bury the used body part in the cemetery and wait for the fruit of death to germinate with full power. The results will manifest themselves in 66 days. If there are no results after 66 days, simply go to the cemetery and banish or encircle the place where the body part was buried, this will close the operation.

Mastery of Nature: We can use a corpse to control a specific person, and in that same way we can direct the powers of Heldrasil to gain strength over the Yggdrasil for our personal benefit. Unlike the previous process, here we channel the powers of Death to favor us in every way. To accomplish this, we use the method described above except that instead of carving our intention with the name of the person in runic we will carve our magickal purpose using High Speech or Harmal. For example, we carve the word "Slátr" upon a piece of flesh that will represent the flesh of Ymir in case our purpose is to prosper. Remember that this should be inscribed in runes (slatr). Performing this work provides a type of specific benefit in our personal universe, but we cannot break the established order in which the corpse of Ymir was dissected. This gradual development is an empowerment method where we slowly channel the Acausal body components of Ymir in a total of nine operations, one for each component or limb of Hrimáifaðir, Frost's grandfather. The nine empowerments can be done with different corpses, each component binds us to the Gríma of the deceased. This produces a link between the practitioner and the deceased. This synergy or convergence potently increases the Hamingja of the practitioner and will subject all beings and inhabitants of the underworld to "listen" and obey more closely.

The operation must be carried out during the New Moon during nine lunar months, stopping the practice can be counterproductive as Death forces need continuity in their channeling and command, otherwise these will consume the Hamingja of the practitioner until exhausting his last Önd. On the other hand, if we complete the nine operations successfully, the unlimited power of the Heldrasil will nourish our Rótsál during the remainder of this incarnation. Those who manage to finish this operation receive the title "Vissnar", Wise of the Corpses. The use of dead animals that have been found by chance (*) applies to this structure, but their energy lasts at most a year and does not replace the initial empowerment; if you are unsure of performing an operation with human corpses, it is suggested to begin practices with dead animals since their Hyde and Grima will only be for one year within your Being.

There is also the possibility of repeating this form of Kvisanár a successive number of times in order to integrate more power into our being and incredibly enhance our Hamingja. However, the Necromancer must take special care choosing the corpses and limbs he is going to work with since they will be integrated with your Self and after that the process is quite difficult (if not impossible) to reverse. Operations should always be performed in the order shown even when you have already completed the first cycle or the first 9 operations. The conversion process in a Víssnár is something that takes time and dedication, and only the most daring Seiðr practitioners reach this goal; those who arrive to the ninth limb receive the Bone Crown of Hel thus becoming authentic necromancers.

Note: The Sparks are interpreted as the eyes of the corpse, this step can be worked as an evocation of the spirit of the deceased to integrate it into your Rótsál and thus close the cycle.

	Body Part	Hármál	Rule Over	Benefit
1	Flesh	Slátr	Earth	Abundance
2	Bones	Bein	Mountains	Fertility
3	Blood	Dreyri	Lakes and Seas	Sexuality
4	Teeth	Tonn	Stones	Prestige
5	Hair	Skör	Trees	Vitality
6	Worms	Ormr	Dwarves	Protection
7	Cranium	Hauss	Sky	Love
8	Skull	Heili	Clouds	Knowledge
9	Sparks	Sparkr	Stars	Power

Kvisavarði – The Mound's Whisper

This procedure is similar to Trollkveðja but in this case we will limit ourselves to the evocatory act. In Nordic culture there are different types of beings from the Helheim or Heldrasil that possess different abilities and skills that can be useful for different functions. Within the traditional spiritual practice of Norse Paganism, calling the spirits of the dead was a taboo or forbidden act; the only valid form of communication with them was through

Blot to honor the memory of those who were no longer with us. Current neo Paganism systems, such as Asatrú and Oðinism, still consider calling the dead as an act of desecration, an offense against the family lineage and scorn towards Odin as he was the one who rescued the souls of warriors killed in battle and carried them to Valhalla. At the end of the XVI century Heleikinn practitioners were caught in the act of communing with the dead; this entailed the death penalty and therefore their execution, an event that befell Sigurdur Jonsson in Þingvellir, Iceland. Currently the development of this Art can be experimented freely and without fear of punishment. Þursatrú goes beyond the limitations imposed by the cosmic order of the Æsir and finds knowledge and wisdom where others only see darkness or evil. Performing evocation to different beings who dwell in the land of death gives us the possibility to obtain information from those who have transcended the Yggdrasil and are now contained in the Heldrasil during their transit through the planes of consciousness. The following is a list of such entities:

Langniðiar - Ancestors: Members of our bloodline who have died and are now in one of the underworlds governed by Hela. The Ancients only possess knowledge and memory of what they did in life. In the moment of death they do not acquire any spiritual gift or ability as many seem to think. The Langniðiar are the Hyde or astral body of every human being who is trapped in the realm of death; when his process of consciousness has been balanced in Hela's kingdom, then their Hyde is released and can continue his way to a future rebirth. Each of our ancestors is a storehouse of information and energy. The closer we are to our own ancestors the more powerful our Hamingja is; they lend us their help and protection.

Skrípi - Spectrum: Spirits of decadent and haunting appearance, their eyes are open and never blink, their skin is completely white. They have gone through the same events of the Ancestors; however, they have decided to willingly stay in Heldrasil at the service of the Guardians that protect each Underworld. The Skrípi are usually the ghosts of human beings who failed to obtain power or growth in life, and in death they perceived the opposite thereby creating an anchor in these planes. The power of a Skrípi depends on how long he or she has been in that plane of the Underworld. Many have wandered during centuries or have established a territory in the Tree of Death. Their power also grows when dragging the people of Midgard/living beings to the Heldrasil; this is why many Necromancers summon them to kill their enemies.

Haugbúi - Mound Dweller: This type of spirit has been through the same experiences of the Langniðiar and the ancestors except that his Hyde never arrived at Heldrasil but remained trapped to the site where he was buried or entombed. Another common epithet for this kind of being is "Sleeping Mound" because it was common for Norse graves to be arranged as a conical mound of stones; these burial mounds were called "Varda" or "Vardi" and were considered by the locals as places to have direct encounters with these shadows of death. The mound or Tomb is then considered sacred for the dwellers of the Tree of Death; each Vardi is an area jealously protected by a dead spirit. The Vardi were generated when a family buried a relative with a treasure, valuables or something representative of their lineage. If a thief or intruder dared to profane said land, then the Haugbúi would violently attack him, initially producing a severe disease and then draining their blood's power until causing death. Something interesting about this is that once unleashed the fury of a Haugbúi cannot be stopped until the thief returns what was stolen or until he is brought to death. We can evoke a Haugbúi at some Vardi using two methods:

Waiting until a relative dies and the day after his funeral call his soul or hyde and proceed to give instructions of what to protect.

Going to a cemetery and finding the soul or Hyde of a deceased who has not found rest; we do this as follows:

- We give an offering of incense and Water to the Guardian of the Cemetery.

- Then proceed to walk slowly through the cemetery with our Kyllrúnar (Runic Bag), and as we stir the runes inside the bag, when we pass in front of a tomb we take a single rune out of the bag. If the rune is Pertra *p* rune, then a Haugbúi is living in that tomb or Vardi; in case of any other rune it is taken as a sign that the tomb is empty, and we place it back inside the Kyllrúnar and continue our trek consulting at each Vardi.

- Should Pertra appear then we make a final consultation to verify that the Haugbúi is not already dedicated to protecting a family treasure or anything of value. We draw another rune from the bag; if Ken *k*, Gifu *g* or Odal *E*, it means that the Haugbúi already has a predetermined task and we cannot interrupt his process. On the other hand, if any other runes appear, then the Haugbúi is free of any work and we can talk with his Spirit. Speaking to him is something that does not have to be complicated; we take note of the data on the tombstone and proceed to evoke him in our personal temple. Once a pact has been established, we return to his grave and leave an object that represents that which we want him to protect.

Such articles can vary, but it is common to leave a bag of coins to protect the economic aspect; others leave the garment of a lover so no one else can come close to him/her or some of the practitioner's hair each month to provide them with physical protection. The possibilities are endless and it all depends of the practitioner's wit.

- **Draugr - Vampire or Ghost:** Of all the creatures that inhabit the realm of death this is the best known in Nordic culture and also the most dangerous and feared. The Draugr are beings that roam the earth in service of Hela by promoting war, hatred and murder. They are responsible for causing a man to kill others or to commit suicide. The Draugr do not act deliberately; they prey on those who have desecrated the land of death or those who have stolen from the dead. Hela also sends Draugr to those who do not appreciate their own life and threaten it in any way. If a Draugr kills a human being, the soul of this will become Draugr and now will serve the Hrimgýgr Hela. There are two types of Draugr, the Vampire and the Ghost, and each one has a particular quality.

- **Draugrstíga - Ghost:** The Ghost Walker or Draugrstíga causes death by depression or discouragement towards life, affects those who do not love their lives and leads to self-destruction through craving to toxins that pollute the body or failed suicide attempts.

- **Draugrblót - Vampire:** The Vampire or Draugrblót causes the death of those who have profaned the dead by taking objects from the cemetery which were not theirs, those who have robbed the dead of their inheritances and lands. The Draugrblót chases humans that are contaminated by anger and whisper in their ears to deprive others of life; when the murderer dies, it turns into a Draugrblót.

There are no methods to create a Draugr but we can call them by their name through a Varð Lokkur and direct their attention toward a person to cause his death. Directing the essence of a Draugr towards another human being is one of the most powerful acts of Heleikinn because once the spirit has been sent there is no method to bring it back. White magic or cosmic magic cannot protect anyone against such beings; only the Leiken can release someone from such a tremendous evil.

There is only one way for a Draugr to cease its task. We should carve on a rock or pine/oak bark the Scandinavian Kalleby Stone Sorcery. She has a spell that has been interpreted and used in different ways. The stone contains this script in Old Futhark:

Þrawijan Haitinaz Was

TrawjJan 2 Iajtjnax 2 was
The first meaning is the literal translation of the Proto-Nordic root expressed as:

The longing has been imposed (on him).

This is one way to establish command or control over this particular spirit. A second translation was done by Nigel Jackson (35) in his study on vampirism which he states as:

(35): **Kalleby Runestone:** Vampiros, Hombres Lobo y los Cambia Pieles, Complete Vampire, Nigel Jackson, 1995.

He (the deceased) was forced to be consummed (in the grave).

The following Galdrastafir or Linked Rune should be drawn in stone or wood and be consecrated through the Trolltaufr Seiðr to the Spirits of Blood and Sleep. The same shall be covered or encircled by three plants which have the power to ward off the Draugr.

- Yellow Rose Petals.
- Sunflower Petals.
- Laurel leaves.

When Galdrastafir has been brought to life through the Trolltaufr Seiðr, we head towards the nearest graveyard and bury the amulet in a tomb or mound in which no Haugbúi resides. The empty tomb will be the home of the Draugr, and he will remain anchored to the land of death. The actions of these spirits can only be contained in this way; they do not recognize other spells, seals, talismans or plants.

Ielejkjn Heleikinn– Necromancy

Rúnarsteinn Kalleby – Kalleby Runic Stone

The Mound's Whisper has simple rules which facilitate the process of summoning the spirits of the dead. The first to consider is the creation of a Vard Lokkur related to different aspects of each of the Spirits, the more accurate and descriptive the more direct the contact will be; remember that this must be whispered and your voice should never be raised when calling the dead. The Vard Lokkur should be a replica of the dying process; therefore, the song should imitate the cry of someone who is dying until abiding in silence. During introspective Heleikinn processes we can pronounce the Vard Lokkur mentally and the music will come from the heart, the core of the whole Like. Destruction or war operations can use some music, but the only musical instruments used to call the inhabitants of Heldrasil are those that have been manufactured in bone, no other should be implemented.

- **Evocation - Incense:** The essence of the Dead is manifested in the air and in the water. We can bring their essence by burning incense with strong and fresh, such as musk, jasmine and coca leaf snuff. In this smoke we can see the manifestation of the Spirit that we called. The operation should be performed facing west, the direction in which the sun dies and darkness manifests.

- **Invocation - Breath:** The power of the spirits of the dead can be internalized through ice and water. This is represented as slow and paused breaths where the heart rate goes down slowly. Visualize the Ancestor, Specter, Ghost, Mound Dweller or Vampire enthroned in your Being. A.O Spare's Death Posture technique is a good way to achieve this kind of invocation.

Recommended items: to evoke the spirits of the dead use only water and ice elements.

Recommended Þursar ok Gýgjar:

-Heiðr (Protects during Evocation practices).
-Rym (Searches and finds any Heldrasil entity).
-Hel (Searches and finds any Heldrasil entity).
-Hela (Gives Knowledge about the realm of the dead, protects during Evocation practices).
-Ammá o Amá (Dominates and controls other beings).
-Leiken (Destroys, curses and kills Guardians, Gods and Protectors of the Cosmos).

Heldrasil Root: Elvidnir. We can travel to Elvidnir's root and learn in Hrimgýgr Hela's library about the higher mysteries related to Heleikinn/Necromancy.

Contributors

ALBERT PETERSEN: Petersen is not interested in the left or the right, the black or the white. Either it Works or it does not. Initiated in the 90s into a system that highlights the inherent limitations and flaws of the mind, Petersen is, among other things, a journalist, anthropologist, magician, hypocrite and fool—though often embittered, he does laugh a lot.

albertpetersen418@gmail.com

ROBERT PODGURSKI: Robert Podgurski has undertaken a lifelong scholarly pursuit investigating the history and genesis of hermeticism, magick, alchemy, the Cabala, and western esoteric studies. During this time he has researched as well as practiced the Enochian system of angelic magic as developed by John Dee and Sir Edward Kelley. In 1981 he discovered an innovative magical tool, the Grid Sigil that has shed light upon and acted as a unifying nexus between his various magical fields of inquiry. This finding has formed the basis for his recently released book: *The Sacred Alignments and Dark Side of Sigils*, published by Mandrake Press Ltd, 2012. Bob has published articles, lectured, and conducted workshops on John Dee, sigil magick, and the Grid Sigil throughout the US. He has also worked extensively with cththonic magick exploring various facets of the Qliphoth. His first grimoire of Lovecraftian-based magick will be published later this summer by Aion Sophia Press. His first collection of poems: *Would-Be Wand* will also be forthcoming from Spuyten Duyvil Press later this year.

For more information go to www.gridmagick.com and www.facebook.com/thesacredalignmentsanddarksideofsigils.

deathsigil@gmail.com

DAVID EOSPHORUS MAPLES: David 'Eosphorus' Maples – My spiritual journey(s) began with Catholicism, the home-taught kind, led to Nichiren Daishonin Buddhism and then evolved to several occult pathways. I began my occult studies within Luciferian Gnosticism—this taught me many things about my subtle bodies, sex magick and traveling. I took what I found of use within this system and moved on. After a time, I became very well acquainted with the Ordo Ascensum Aetyrnalis, reaching some of its highest degrees before its eventual downfall. Soon after, I was approached with an offer to become initiated into the Haitian Voudon mysteries by a very powerful Houngan who noticed the spirits congregated around me. He informed me that my guardian spirits were very hot and called for very particular ceremonies, secret ceremonies. I could not deny such a gift. Since becoming initiated, I have served mostly the Petro Loa and the Ghuede, plus a few secret families of Loa. It is in my star of destiny to spread a Black Flame across the whole of the community.

A culmination of the lessons I have learned from these ancient ancestors is being released to the public through the masterful binding of Nephilim Press (nephilimpress.com). It is for the Black Brothers of the Flame that this work is being released, and it is for those Black Brothers that I weep. The burden of the hot spirits is a heavy one, a constant refining through fire, but our kind is strong. It is time to release the bonds and shatter the hall of mirrors. Memento Mori…

David is also an initiate of the Double Current of the Horus/Maat Lodge. 93 696!

David can be contacted through his personal email address: dravex6493@gmail.com

ISABELLE GABORIT: I am an occult artist who relentlessly tries to catch a glimpse of the Unseen through the mediums of paint and inks, tapping into that Force within and without, giving it Form. As an illustrator I have been collaborating with a number of occult writers creating visual forms to enhance their words and ideas. My artistic endeavours run parallel to, and very often overlap with, my practise of the Magical Arts. In my work I stand at that threshold; each work becomes a journey, starting with a blank page or canvas and a kernel of an idea; then a leap into the unknown as I jump from one layer to the other, from one media to the next, exploring, trusting the unknown and unfamiliar. I have been fortunate to have had my work commissioned for occult Books and publications worldwide. My work has been exhibited extensively nationally and internationally, including Northern Ireland, Spain, China and France.

You can get updates on my artistic projects at:
https://www.facebook.com/isabelle.gaborit.artist
and purchase limited editions fine Art prints of my illustrations at:
http://www.etsy.com/shop/Sibealscave
isabellegaborit@gmail.com

S. CONNOLLY: S. Connelly has been practicing and studying all things "occult" and metaphysical since 1984. Her interest started with divination, gematria, and necromancy and quickly spiraled toward ceremonial magick, witchcraft, and Daemons. She has been a practicing Daemonolatress since 1988.

For more about S. Connolly: http://www.s-connolly.com
For more about Daemonolatry: http://www.demonolatry.org
swordarkeereon@gmail.com

SEAN WOODWARD: Sean Woodward is an initiate of OTOA-LCN and has created the Carrefour Tarot in service to the Monastery of the Seven Rays and the establishment of the Evolving Empire of the Hoodoo Spirits. He was a member of the Nephthys Arachna Power Zone and holds the charter of Knight Diplomatis Supreme of Society OTO. His art and writing have been published internationally, appearing in Lamp of Thoth, Zhoupheus and Estronomicon. He is represented by ZOSHOUSE | FINE-ART and his tarot and art may be purchased at www.seanwoodward.com.

t3kton@gmail.com

MATTHEW WIGTHMAN: Besides being the Editor on the English edition of *Fosforos*—due out from Ixaxaar this September—Matthew Wightman's background is primarily an academic one. He holds a bachelor's degree in Religious Studies and a master's degree in Theology awarded from Yale and is currently pursuing a doctoral degree in Theology and Philosophical Studies at a university in the United States. He identifies himself as an Anti-cosmic Satanist / Gnostic Luciferian and follows the Current 218.

serpentofeden@gmail.com

EDGAR KERVAL: Edgar Kerval, from Colombia, South America – Musician, writer and artist focused on deconstructing different magickal vortices through deep states of consciousness and gnosis, which are reflected in his ritual projects, such as EMME YA, in which he focuses atavism and chthonic energies to create vast soundscapes and ritual vaporous atmospheres. Also working on other projects, such as THE RED PATH, THE RED ANGLE, NOX 210, :ARCHAIC:, SONS OV SIRIUS, LUX ASTRALIS, TOTEM ... to name a few. Edgar Kerval published his book *Via Siniestra* -under the mask of the red gods- through Aeon Sophia Press. In which he recorded his experiences with Qliphotic magick and energies from African and Brazilian sorcery which he called "The Red Gods".

He also worked in publications such as *Qliphoth Journal* and *Sabbatica*. Also, he is working on his second book coming out in 2014, published by Nephilim Press.

    www.qliphothjournal.blogspot.com
    www.sunbehindthesun.blogspot.com
    Kerval111@gmail.com

ASENATH MASON: Asenath Mason is a writer and graphic designer. Author of essays on esoteric, religious and mythological subjects, with a particular focus on the Left Hand Path philosophy. Active practitioner of Occult Arts. Founder and coordinator of the Temple of Ascending Flame. Author of *The Book of Mephisto: A Modern Grimoire of the Faustian Tradition* (2006), *Necronomicon Gnosis: A Practical Introduction* (2007), *Sol Tenebrarum: The Occult Study of Melancholy* (2011), *The Grimoire of Tiamat* (2013), and co-author of *Glimpses of the Left Hand Path* (2004), and *Exploring the Unnamable: Wanderings in the Labyrinths of Zin* (2007). She is also a varied artist, working with digital media, and themes of her artwork include gothic, fantasy and esoteric concepts.

    Contact: www.facebook.com/asenath.mason
    http://ascendingflame.com/

DAEMON BARZAI: Daemon Barzai is a Draconian Magician. Devotee to the Great Old Ones. Esoteric Translator, Writer and Publisher. Author of *The Nyarlathotep Book* (2013).

    Website:
    www.diariodeunbrujo.com.ar
    www.blacktowerpublishing.com.ar

Contributors

Rafal Kosela:
Web: www.loveartmagick.blogspot.com
E-mail: therion.trismegistos@gmail.com

Kyle Fite: Kyle Fite is an Artist, Writer and Social Worker operating between the American Midwest and Zothyria. In addition to presently serving OTOA-LCN as its Sovereign Grand Master, he is a proud member of the Typhonian Order and a devoted enthusiast of the work of E.J. Gold. His ongoing series BECOMING HOODOO is forming the framework of a book by the same name as it is serialized through a variety of publications. The total vision of this work is one of coming to the Crossroads between the Finite and Transcendental. Ultimately, it is intended to be an Initiatory Crucifixion & Resurrection via the means of Literary Device.
kylefite@yahoo.com

Barry William Hale: Australian Artist and Occultist.

His works have been exhibited internationally and within Australia along side of such Occult emissaries as Aleister Crowley, Austin Osman Spare and Rosaleen Norton to name a few. He has also been privileged to be published alongside of authors of the Western Esoteric Tradition that inspired him in his youth.

His works have been described as 'largely responsible for the current rediscovery of the esoteric as a valid and important part of art history.'

As an Artist and Author his work inhabits a liminal zone between Art and the Occult.

As an occult practitioner his praxis is the primary source of his interdisciplinary research and creative output. His Art being the residue that is produced by the collusion of this occult praxis and art process.

Hale's work is expressed through a variety of mediums and modes of creative output. From more traditional art making to new media, such as painting, drawing and sculpture, to installation, video, sound and writing. Hale is also part of the artistic and magical collaboration NOKO, whose work blurs the line between Performance and Magical Ritual.

His work and collaborations have been represented at the 17th Australian Biennale and the Adelaide Fringe Festival, Window to the Sacred, & IMAGE exhibitions to performances at the Equinox Festival and the Esoteric Book Conference with NOKO.

He is represented by Fulgur Esoterica who have been instrumental in the promulgation of Esoteric Art and publishing for 20 years, and a pioneer of the Talismanic Book.

And he is also by Buratti Fine Arts who represent some of Australia's most prominent Artists.

He is currently working on a multimedia project HYPRKUB210 with Fulgur Esoteric and a major exhibition 'Window to the Sacred' which will be touring Nationally in Australia until 2016.

He is also a writer who has been published by Fulgur Esoterica and was instrumental in the production of the 'Waratah Journal' of the Australian O.T.O. which has been an acknowledged inspiration to other Art/Occult Journals.

http://www.barrywilliamhale.com/
http://fulgur.co.uk/artists/barry-william-hale/

MATTHEW VENUS: an artist, sigilic magician, magical apothecary, rootworker, and witch. His writings and talismanic pieces are often a reflection of his unique magical praxis and the spirits with whom he works. Along with his partner, he owns and operates Spiritus Arcanum, an online occult shop specializing in handcrafted and magically empowered artwork, jewelry, and apothecary items. www.spiritusarcanum.com.

xexos45@yahoo.com

MICA GRIES: was born in Los Angeles, California in the early spring of 1980. He now lives on a small, rural island in British Columbia, Canada with his wife, black cat and two Jack Russel Terrorists. Mica has been an avid student of the occult for many years, even going so far as to turn a corner of his bedroom into an alchemical laboratory (much to the frustration of his poor wife).

He began writing in high school, enflamed by the Mercuric urge when a short, impromptu poem on his adolescent crush turned into a three-page epic on shamanic initiation. After riding the waves of poetry and streams-of-consciousness for many years, Mica finally turned to the more disciplined art of fiction and essay writing. He has an essay published in the anthology *The Immanence of Myth* on the Dionysian experience. Mica is currently working on a book of short stories, in the genre of dark occult fiction, to be published by Nephilim Press.

mtgries@telus.net

LJÓSSÁL LOÐURSSON: Ljóssál Loðursson is a Humuy Camayok or Great Sorcerer empowered in traditional indigenous medicine by Gilberto Zuñina Tenganan (Taita Yahuasca) of the ethnicity of Los Pastos. Active renovator of a Shakta current in the Andinous territory, founder of the Arcanum Ordo Nigri Solis or the Secret Order of the Black Sun in Latin America. He has worked actively with initiatory and magickal orders as the Ordo Templi Orientis and the Astrum Argentum. He serves as an emissary of the Plutonian currents for the independent tantric lineage Surya Abhinila in the process towards Awakening and Liberation of Consciousness. His path focuses on Nordic Paganism of the Left Hand Path called Þursatrú, His books have an orientation toward Gnostic Cainite traditions based in Sinister Alchemy and the exploration of the night side of the Self. He has also been precursor of esoteric events, such as Magick Camps and Magick Fest.

nekelmoth@hotmail.com

THE NYARLATHOTEP BOOK

THE CRAWLING CHAOS

Daemon Barzai

Several people know his name, although only a few understand how to work with him. Nyarlathotep: The Crawling Chaos is the messenger of the Great Old Ones, an emissary between humans and the Outer Gods. He is a deity with a thousand faces. This ritual book explains how to work with him in a theoretical and workable approach. This Grimoire has been inspired by Nyarlathotep himself. Here, you will discover things that have never been published before.

The book will cover such themes as: Who Nyarlathotep really is, Invocation and Evocation of Nyarlathotep, The Mirror of Queen Nitocris, The Labyrinths of Kish, The Black Tower of Koth, A Ritual of Possessions, A Pact with Nyarlathotep, The Masks of Nyarlathotep, Nyarlathotep as a Black Man of the Sabbat and much more...

www.blacktowerpublishing.com

Visions of the Nightside

Temple of Ascending Flame

Visions of the Nightside is a collection of essays, rituals and various expressions of personal gnosis written by members and associates of the Temple of Ascending Flame. Unique and evocative in its content and form, the book comprises powerful manifestations of magical practice with the forces of the Nightside: dark Gods and Goddesses, primal energies of the Void, entities residing on the Qlipothic Tree, demons of infernal regions, and spirits from a whole range of traditions. It is a practical research and insight into the practice of the Left-Hand-Path magic within the modern context, with contributions from working magicians and initiates of Draconian and Atlantean traditions.

www.blacktowerpublishing.com

Keys Of Ocat

Ms. Connolly's 13th book reveals the never before published Saturn rites, seals, and theophantic gate opening rituals of Ocat, the abyssal gatekeeper of the dead. Behind His gates dwell the Daemons of death, including Euronymous, Balberith, Bune, Hekate, Frucisierre, and many others. These blood magick rituals, talismans and seals will aid the advanced magician in conjuring Daemons to speak with the dead, commune with death, and discover the true meaning of mortality and spiritual immortality. Be forewarned, however, Ocat is not known to be a friendly gatekeeper to all magi who approach Him, and the Daemons behind His gates are some of the most terrifying of their nature.

This book is available through www.nephilimpress.com

www.ingramcontent.com/pod-product-compliance
Lightning Source LLC
Chambersburg PA
CBHW032055090426
42744CB00005B/221